Prayer

Discover the secret to effective fasting and prayer

Guillermo Maldonado

Our Mission

Called to bring the supernatural power of God to this generation.

Prayer

ISBN: 978-1-59272-090-3
Third Edition 2007

Project Director: Addilena Torres
Translation: Adriana Cardona
Interior Design: Adriana Cardona
Cover Design: ERJ Publications

ERJ Publications
13651 SW 143 Ct., Suite 101, Miami, FL 33186
Tel: (305) 382-3171 - Fax: (305) 675-5770

Category: Prayer

Printed in the United States of America

Dedication

I dedicate this book to my wife Ana for her total support of this ministry; you are my ideal helper in life. Thank you for your prayers; my appreciation for you is eternal.

I also dedicate this book to my sons Bryan and Ronald, who, together with my wife, inspire me to keep going in ministry. After Him, you are the greatest treasures God has given me!

Acknowledgements

I would like to thank every person who has helped me to grow and who inspires me to become a better leader, giving it all in prayer to make this book a reality.

To my intercessors: Sarahi, Piedad, Diana, Gisela, Clarita, Linda, Nadgee, Anita, and the rest of the early morning prayer team; thank you for your prayers, not only for me, but for the ministry as well.

To the GM International team, thank you for making the publication of this book a reality.

Index

Introduction

The purpose of this book is to help you, the reader, develop a close and intimate relationship with God. Because of it, as you read this book, you will be able to discover a series of useful suggestions that will become a great blessing, if you choose to use them in your daily living.

You will also find a valuable treasure that will allow you to step into deeper levels of prayer and help you enjoy your prayer time as you practice it.

Since prayer is not an option for the believer, but a commandment, we must learn to develop strategies that improve our intimacy with God. This is essential and greatly needed to achieve the level of spiritual maturity that will help us to be successful, not only in our ministries, but in all facets of life.

1

Intimate Communion with God

Before we begin to develop, in detail, this study on prayer, it is necessary to emphasize the fundamental reason we pray, which is to have an intimate relationship with God. It is to know Him, His ways, why He does the things He does, and how He does them. If I were to say this in one phrase, I would have to say, it is to know God's deepest secrets.

In this study, we will take a look at every principal aspect of prayer, beginning with an intimate communion with Him.

God's desire has always been to have intimate communion with His people. At the beginning of creation, in the book of Genesis, the Word teaches that God walked and talked with Adam in the Garden of Eden. However, when sin came, man also sinned against God, breaking his communion with Him. Now, man is unable to communicate with God because his spirit is in darkness. Because of man's downfall, God provided for his salvation by sending His Son, Jesus Christ, born of a virgin, to be crucified, raised on the third day, and who now sits at the right hand of the Father. Through His sacrifice, man's communion with the Father is restored once again. He removed our heart of stone and replaced it with a heart of flesh.

What is the main purpose of prayer?

There are many reasons, which we will deal with later, but the main reason prayer exists is to give us an opportunity to have communion with Him. Let us take a closer look at this subject.

What is communion?

The word communion in the Greek language is "*koinonia*", meaning to have something in common, fellowship, participation, friendship, communication and dialogue. Therefore, communion with God is to have friendship, dialogue and fellowship with Him, establishing a close relationship, because this is His desire.

Who does God desire to have communion with?

- **He desires to have intimate communion with those who fear Him.**

  "[14]The secret of the LORD is with those who fear Him, and He will show them His covenant." Psalms 25.14

  What is fear of God?

  The words, "fear of God" in Hebrew mean feeling a terror to please Him and a terror of displeasing Him. In modern terminology, the words "fear of God" can be defined as loving everything God loves and hating everything God hates.

  In the beginning, communion was defined as having something in common, fellowship, friendship, participation and to be in society with. This communion is found between God and those who dread displeasing Him. If our desire is to please God, then we must be aware of those things God hates in order for us to develop a close relationship with Him. Many believers try to establish an intimate relationship with God, but still live in sin; they have secrets God disapproves of.

What does God hate?

Following is a list of seven sins the Bible teaches that God hates:

"[16]These six things the LORD hates, yes, seven are an abomination to Him: [17]A proud look, a lying tongue, hands that shed innocent blood, [18] a heart that devises wicked plans, feet that are swift in running to evil, [19] a false witness who speaks lies,and one who sows discord among brethren." Proverbs 6.16-19

1. A proud look.
2. A lying tongue.
3. Hands that shed innocent blood.
4. A heart that devises wicked plans.
5. Feet that are swift in running to evil.
6. The false witness who speaks lies.
7. One who sows discord among the brethren.

Obviously, there are many more things God hates, but these seven are the root of other sins. The more we hate evil and everything sin stands for, the closer our relationship with Him will be. But, on the contrary, if we have few things in common with God, the weaker our relationship with Him will be. What we have in common with God will bring us closer to Him. If our desire is to have an intimate relationship with Him, we must hate what He hates and love what He loves.

- **His communion is also with the righteous.** The word "righteous" in Hebrew is "*yashar*", which means direct, straight, right before God's eyes, not double minded and morally correct.

If we were to apply this to our daily living, we could say: intimate communion with the Lord is with those who are morally honorable, who hunger and thirst for righteousness, and who are blameless before Him. It is clearly written in the Holy Scriptures that God can not have fellowship with individuals living in sin; therefore, to have a close relationship with God, it is essential to live right, eliminate sin, and seek holiness.

Communion with Him is our priority

Unfortunately, we see men and women who were once greatly used by God, but suddenly stumbled and fell into sin. We have seen believers who are on "fire" for Him and, from one minute to the next, they simply walk away. Then the question is: "What happened?" The answer to every question turns out to be the neglect of their communion and relationship with Him.

Thousands of believers attend church every Sunday. They sit in their seats, but do not have any personal relationship with Him. Their prayer life and reading of the Word is practically non-existent. They lack the vision of God and have no idea what God's will and purpose is for their lives. Some are living in sin and have no idea who God is. Yes, they received Him as Lord and Savior, but after this, they neglected to establish that relationship with Him; as a result, they live in wretchedness and defeat; everything goes wrong. Our communion and rela-tionship with God is priceless and should be a priority in our lives.

What is a moral value?

A moral value or standard is a biblical belief we practice daily. If our relationship with God is a moral value in our lives, then we should be seeking His face and praying everyday. For example, we understand that physical exercise is good for us and establish it as being a moral value in our lives, but if we do not practice it, it is not a moral value. Our relationship with God is the same way; we should never walk out of our homes without first spending time with Him. Prayer teaches us to be totally dependent on Him.

What is a priority?

A priority is anything to which we give first place, in order of importance; it is that which is most productive and beneficial to us. For example, when prayer is a priority, it implies that before any other responsibility (family and church, among many), we make the effort to have communion with Him.

Communion with God is very important; through it, we communicate with Him. You know someone loves you when they say it; there is great power and action behind these words. Communication is part of God's nature, His desire is to have fellowship with us and to share with us His will and purpose.

The first calling of every believer is to have an intimate communion with God. This is the number one priority and the most difficult one to keep because those who are around do not help in any way to be closer to Him; rather, they become angry when they are not the center of attention.

The main reason we pray and study the Bible is not to receive blessings, but to know Him better. Most people are unable to uphold their intimate communion with God. The number one reason for this is that nothing meaningful or special happens during prayer time; it is not as exciting as expected. There are people who expect to experience thunder and lightning during prayer time, but this is not the way it is. At times, we might have supernatural experiences, but this is not the norm.

Prayer and communion with God, at times, feels like eating cereal without milk. Figuratively speaking, when this happens during prayer time, we must continue our search until we find the "milk". My advice is to diminish your expectations, continue reading the Word, even if nothing special happens, and eventually, the wonderful manifestation of His presence will be evident.

"One thing is necessary"

"[38]Now it happened as they went that He entered a certain village; and a certain woman named Martha welcomed Him into her house. [39]And she had a sister called Mary, who also sat at Jesus' feet and heard His word. [40]But Martha was **distracted** *with much serving, and she approached Him and said, "Lord, do You not care that my sister has left me to serve alone? Therefore tell her to help me. [41]And Jesus answered and said to her, "Martha, Martha, you are worried and troubled about many things. [42]But one thing is needed, and Mary has chosen that good part, which will not be taken away from her." Luke 10.38-42*

The word "distracted" means to be absorbed or going around in circles. There are different theories based on this part of Scripture. Some think we must have Martha and Maria in the body of Christ, one to serve and the other to be spiritual. However, I personally believe, according to what Jesus says and does concerning Martha, that we do not need this type of Marthas in the church because Jesus, in no way, approves her kind of service.

We understand that serving God is important, but not the way Martha does it, where service comes before our relationship with God. Martha says to Jesus, "Tell her to help me." It is human nature to judge others according to our measure of service or commitment, while others do not serve using these same criteria. Martha complains to Jesus that Maria is not helping her, but His response is, "Martha, Martha…" When Jesus calls someone by name, not once, but twice, He does it for two reasons: to express His great love towards that person and to discipline and correct. *One thing is necessary,* to be in communion with God, to feel His love and have an intimate relationship with Him. When we feel His love we are self-assured, we rejoice in the success of others and we do not covet or feel envy towards others. Some are addicted to sports or food, but it is better to be addicted to His presence. We should be addicted to His presence! We should all desire to be with Him, and our heart should yearn for a close relationship with Him.

Jesus' prayer life and His communion with the Father

Let us analyze His prayer life and learn from Him.

"12Now it came to pass in those days that He went out to the mountain to pray, and continued all night in prayer to God." Luke 6.12

"23And when He had sent the multitudes away, He went up on the mountain by Himself to pray. Now when evening came, He was alone there." Matthew 14.23

We must understand the nature of His prayer. He prayed all the time, and even though He was the Son of God, He had a close relationship with the Father. His prayers were all for Him; prayer was a moral value and a priority in His life.

When did Jesus pray?

- **Jesus prayed in the morning.** His morning prayers show us that His priority was to spend time in communion with the Father; this was the first thing He did.

  "35Now in the morning, having risen a long while before daylight, He went out and departed to a solitary place; and there He prayed." Mark 1.35

- **Jesus prayed at night.** After spending time ministering, praying for the sick, casting out demons, and preaching the Word, Jesus knew He was left empty because He had given everything He had. This is the reason He prayed.

  "12Now it came to pass in those days that He went out to the mountain to pray, and continued all night in prayer to God." Luke 6.12

- **Jesus prayed in the afternoon.** Once again, it is clear that Jesus had an attitude of prayer all day long.

  "23And when He had sent the multitudes away, He went up on the mountain by Himself to pray. Now when evening came, He was alone there." Matthew 14.23

Notice that every time Jesus prayed, He was alone. This demonstrates that prayer is something personal with God. Even though Jesus is the Son of God, He prayed all the time. In His example, we are able to see His total dependence on the Father through prayer. If He found it necessary to do it, even thought He is the Son of God, then we, as men and women with defects and shortcomings, also need to pray. We must live in daily communion with the Father.

There are a few questions we might ask concerning Jesus' prayer life:

- Did Jesus pray with anybody? He prayed alone, separate from everybody, and with His disciples. We should also have time alone with God and time of prayer with others.

  "28Now it came to pass, about eight days after these sayings, that He took Peter, John, and James and went up on the mountain to pray. 29As He prayed, the appearance of His face was altered, and His robe became white and glistening." Luke 9.28, 29

- Where did He pray? He would separate Himself from the crowds to pray in the desert, the valley or in the mountains. These days, people do not enjoy prayer if they are uncomfortable, but Jesus prayed regardless of the circumstances or the weather; He prayed anywhere.

  "16So He Himself often withdrew into the wilderness and prayed." Luke 5.16

  Some people think that Jesus had a special air conditioned room where He went to pray, but this is not the case. He prayed in the desert, where nights are cold and the days are hot.

- How long did Jesus pray? He prayed from one hour to all night long. He also prayed during the day. His prayer life went from one to eight hours a day, as far as we can learn from Scripture.

  What did Jesus pray? Our Father...

"[1]Now it came to pass, as He was praying in a certain place, when He ceased, that one of His disciples said to Him, "Lord, teach us to pray, as John also taught his disciples." Luke 11.1

The example that Jesus gave of a prayer is a guide for us to follow when we pray and not words to be repeated over and over again.

What did Jesus teach His disciples concerning prayer? When we take a close look at Jesus' prayer life, we can conclude the following: He was in constant prayer, at all times, and He did it everywhere He was. He prayed for long periods of time, alone, apart from people, or with His disciples. Prayer (communion with His Father) was a priority, a moral value in His life. If communion with God was a priority to Jesus, then how much more should it be for us?

How can we apply this to our lives?

If we seek His face, everything else will be added unto us. If our priority is to seek a close relationship with Him, then everything will come our way. We should regard prayer as a priority and our relationship with Him should be the most important thing in our lives.

"[33]But seek first the kingdom of God and His righteousness and all these things shall be added to you." Matthew 6.33

What are the benefits to having a close relationship with God?

1. **We will have peace**

"[21]Now acquaint yourself with Him, and be at peace; thereby good will come to you." Job 22.21

The word "peace" in Hebrew is "*shalom*", meaning to be sure, complete, strengthened, prosperous and in abundance. In other words, this verse is telling us that our peace is the result of a close relationship with Him. Absence of peace with God is the result of a weak prayer life.

2. Signs and wonders

"[32]Those who do wickedly against the covenant he shall corrupt with flattery; but the people who know their God shall be strong, and carry out great exploits." Daniel 11.32

The meaning of the word **"know"** is an interesting one. In Hebrew this word is "*yada*", meaning to have intimacy with, or have intimate relationships with. The idea behind this word is easily understood when two people rest their heads on a pillow and are able to see each other face to face, making it possible to speak. From the previous verse, we can conclude that people having close relationships with God can stand firm and perform signs and wonders. What is the conclusion? God is only able to do signs and wonders, daring feats, and miracles through us if we have a close relationship with Him. This is why there are only a few men and women through whom God is able to do great wonders; the others have lost their communion with Him and have been doing the work on their own strength. When the apostles were threatened to stop preaching, the only thing they asked for was boldness. This is the Greek word "*parrehesia*", which means to speak with boldness and courage. For anyone to do powerful things for God, it is necessary to have boldness, audacity and the courage to speak.

Audacity, boldness and to speak with courage is a virtue that comes as a result of our close relationship with God and not from human effort.

3. **We will be satisfied and complete**

" [25]For I have satiated the weary soul, and I have replenished every sorrowful soul." Jeremiah 31.25

When Jesus spoke, He said, "Blessed". This word in Greek is *"makarios"*, which means blessed, joyful to be sent forth, spiritually prosperous, alive, with joy and peace, and completely satisfied with God's favor regardless of adverse circumstances. If Jesus said these things about us, then we need to ask ourselves, "Why are many believers feeling dissatisfied and incomplete?" The answer to this question is because the feeling of completeness and satisfaction is the result of a close relationship with God. He is the only one able to fill our emptiness when we are experiencing sadness. He is the only one who can fulfill and satisfy our soul when we feel unloved by our families. He is the only one who can fill the emptiness caused by lack of love; only God can do these things, but only when we have a close relationship with Him. Before we can feel complete, self-assured, secure, at peace, and satisfied, it is necessary to establish a relationship with God.

"[23]which is His body, the fullness of Him who fills all in all." Ephesians 1.23

How can we establish a close relationship with God?

1. We must humble ourselves before His presence.

When we humble ourselves before the presence of God, we are recognizing that our relationship was lacking intimacy and that we are in need of His grace and favor to be able to accomplish the things which He is asking us to do. When we humble ourselves, we are also recognizing that we are weak and that most of what we have accomplished, we have done with human strength, without depending on Him.

"[14]if My people who are called by My name will humble themselves, and pray and seek My face, and turn from their wicked ways, then I will hear from heaven, and will forgive their sin and heal their land." 2 Chronicles 7.14

2. We must begin to pray immediately.

"[21]Now acquaint yourself with Him, and be at peace; thereby good will come to you. [22]Receive, please, instruction from His mouth, And lay up His words in your heart. [23]If you return to the Almighty, you will be built up; you will remove iniquity far from your tents. [24]Then you will lay your gold in the dust, and the gold of Ophir among the stones of the brooks. [25]Yes, the Almighty will be your gold and your precious silver; [26]for then you will have your delight in the Almighty, and lift up your face to God. [27]You will make your prayer to Him, He will hear you, and you will pay your vows." Job 22.21-27

I believe that there is no better time to begin to pray and to seek His face than right now. We must stop talking about prayer and begin to practice it daily.

3. We must seek His face.

The expression *"seek My face"* means to investigate, inquire into, to ascertain, to seek something with diligence, to desperately look for something. I feel that the body of Christ only seeks God in the way mentioned above, for instance, when they are going through crisis or experiencing persecution. Until such a time of desperate need, they sit comfortably and don't bother to seek Him wholeheartedly. The perfect example of someone who seeks God desperately is David, as the following verse reveals:

"1As the deer pants for the water brooks, so pants my soul for You, O God. 2My soul thirsts for God, for the living God. When shall I come and appear before God? Psalms 42.1, 2

"1O God, You are my God; early will I seek You; my soul thirsts for You; my flesh longs for You in a dry and thirsty land where there is no water. 2So I have looked for You in the sanctuary, to see Your power and Your glory. 3Because Your lovingkindness is better than life, my lips shall praise You." Psalms 63.1-3

We can now conclude that one main reason for prayer is to have a close and intimate relationship with God. Humanity was created precisely for this reason: to have and to maintain an eternal relationship with God. It is important to keep in mind that God establishes a relationship with those who fear Him; with those who love what He loves and who hate what He hates, and those who are morally honest. To establish a solid and intimate relationship with Him, should be a priority and a moral value to us, as it was for Jesus. Although He was and is the Son of God, He prayed at all times, during the day and/or night. It is important to understand that our relationship with God will bring us peace, boldness and audacity to accomplish great things for Him. But, above all, our close relationship with Him, will lead us to a place where we will feel completely satisfied and at peace in all areas of our lives. Never depend on external circumstances, nor on the people that are around you, to make you feel happy and content. God is all-sufficient!

2

The Purpose of Prayer

What is the purpose of prayer?

One problem that I see in the body of Christ is the absence of prayer. The meeting with the lowest attendance rate is the prayer meeting. Therefore, we need to ask ourselves, "Why aren't people praying?" I believe the answer is found in the following two reasons:

1. **People do not understand the purpose of prayer.**

   What is the purpose of prayer?

   Before we answer this question, we must first define the word **"purpose"**, which means the original intention for which something was created.

   The first reason why believers do not pray is because they are unaware of the reason why God created prayer. When we ignore this fundamental truth, prayer is misused or practiced without vision or direction.

2. **People do not pray because they don't see satisfactory or positive results.**

   When we ignore the reason for prayer, the desire to do it is automatically lost. In view of this, the results of prayer are negative or non-existent because we pray without understanding why we should do it.

Why should we pray? If God is powerful and does whatever He wants, then what is the purpose of prayer? Why should we pray if God is sovereign and does what He pleases? Why should we pray if God is unaffected by what we do? Why should we pray if God knows everything? Why should we pray if God controls and predetermines everything? What is the reason for prayer, if the devil has already been defeated? Why pray for the lost if it is God's will that we should all be saved?

These are valid questions, and to answer them we must first understand the true nature of God and His desire for humanity. Understanding who God is will guide us to the purpose of prayer. God is a God of purpose. Everything He created on earth, including man, was created to fulfill His purpose.

There are three main reasons why God created man:

1. **Man was created to reflect God's nature and to have a close relationship with Him.**

"26 Then God said, "Let Us make man in Our image, according to Our likeness; let them have dominion over the fish of the sea, over the birds of the air, and over the cattle, over all the earth and over every creeping thing that creeps on the earth." Genesis 1.26

If we were created to reflect God's nature and to enjoy a personal relationship with Him, then this means that we were created with His nature and moral character. The way we develop this image and character is through our close relationship with Him. We will never reflect who He is nor will we feel completely satisfied until we achieve that close relationship with Him. This is the reason why God created us: to reflect His character, love, mercy, compassion, righteousness, peace, authority and His power. These things can never be evident unless a close relationship with Him exists.

2. **God created humanity to fulfill His plans, His purpose and His will on earth.**

God created man in His image and gave him the ability to choose and make decisions for himself. This means that man was given free will to take action and to fulfill the will of God on earth.

God created man with the ability to function on earth, thus giving him legal rights, freedom and authority to operate in it and to have lordship over all creation.

God implemented His will on earth with man's cooperation. This never changed, even after man's downfall.

3. **God created man to have dominion over all things.**

In Genesis 1.26 God said, "*Let them have dominion.*" In this verse, God is giving men the legal right to take dominion and authority to live on earth and to govern over it.

How did God give man the ability to take dominion?

First, God created man with a spirit that came directly from Him; hence, the human race had no choice but to govern the physical world. God gave man a physical body, which is manifested in two genders: masculine and feminine. Man is the only created being that can take dominion of the earth. If something does not have a body and soul, it is illegal. It was precisely because of this reason that God had to come to earth in a physical body.

From the beginning, God established in His Word that the only one with the legal right to take dominion on earth is man, who lives in a physical body.

God created man in His image; that image and likeness is developed through a close and intimate relationship with Him. God created man to fulfill His purpose on earth, to have lordship over all creation, and this is to be done through man's will and the physical body. God is unable to do anything that goes against His Word. Therefore, there are three things He established from the beginning, as we read in Genesis 1.26.

- God is sovereign, as His Word is sovereign.
- God limits Himself with His Word. He is unable to go beyond what He has said or established.
- God never violates His own Word. Everything God declares is law.

Prayer was created and limited by the Word. God established in His Word that for something to be done on earth, it must be done through a physical body and through the spirit.

God is not able to come to earth without a physical body. If He were to do this, He would be contradicting Himself and His Word; this would be illegal on His part because He said in His Word that the human race, with a physical body, would rule and take dominion over the earth. If anyone tries to come to earth without a physical body, he would be illegal. Therefore, God, as well as the devil, needs a physical body to dwell on earth. This is the reason why God said to the devil, "I will come to earth legally, and I will step on your head, and I will do it through a woman."

"[15] And I will put enmity between you and the woman, and between your seed and her Seed; He shall bruise your head, and you shall bruise His heel." Genesis 3.15

How did God enter the earth with a physical body?

- God became Emmanuel. This name means "God with us."

God said to Maria, "I need a physical body because I need to come to earth legally. In simpler terms, God said to the devil, "The woman will be your worst nightmare."

God is unable to interfere in any situation on earth without the prayer of the believer. Prayer is the equivalent of man giving God the legal right to do His will on earth.

God does not use us because we are intelligent, indispensable or great. God uses us because He is trapped and limited by His own Word.

"[18] Assuredly, I say to you, whatever you bind on earth will be bound in heaven, and whatever you loose on earth will be loosed in heaven." Matthew 18.18

When we pray, we give God permission to invade our lives, to change our family, cities and nations.

God desires to heal us, not only to make us feel better, but because He needs us to fulfill His will.

God is looking for someone who lives in a physical body to stand in the gap for His people and pray.

"30 So I sought for a man among them who would make a wall, and stand in the gap before Me on behalf of the land, that I should not destroy it; but I found no one." Ezekiel 22.30

God is seeking a spirit, within a body, to stand in on someone else's behalf. In other words, God is looking for a man or a woman willing to stand in the gap for His people; to build a fortress; to be a covering for a church or a family; and much more. God is saying to us that He needs someone to give birth to His plans here on earth. His desire is to save, heal and to bring revival to our land. God wants to transform our families, but He needs a man that will allow Him to do these things.

Many of God's plans and purposes may never be fulfilled here on earth because there is no one to intercede; there is no one who will take the time to pray for His plans and for His perfect will to be done. Prayer is not on option; it is a must.

"1 Then He spoke a parable to them, that men always ought to pray and not lose heart." Luke 18.1

We are co-laborers with God

"1 We then, as workers together with Him also plead with you not to receive the grace of God in vain." 2 Corinthians 6.1

The word **"workers"** means a group of people that cooperate, help and work together. We need to see humanity as being a part of, and co-laborer with God, to fulfill His plans and purpose. Jesus fulfilled the will of the Father through prayer. The disciples only asked one thing of Jesus; it was to teach them how to pray. They did not ask to be taught how to perform miracles or cast out demons, they asked to be taught how to pray. Why? Because they saw what was happening in the life of Jesus and they understood that everything that He was able to accomplish had to do with His total dependence on His Father through prayer. The disciples knew the secret to His success; it was His prayer life.

Jesus' secret to the success of His ministry was His prayer life.

Jesus would pray for five hours and later only needed two seconds to heal the blind man. I want you to notice the following principle: Jesus spent hours doing one thing and seconds doing another. He continually operated in this way. He spent hours interceding and a minute casting out demons and healing the lepers. The church has yet to understand this truth. We do things the other way around: spend a few minutes with God and later take many hours ministering to the people, in His name. Jesus rebuked demons in a minute by saying, "leave" and the demon left, but what most people don't realize is that in the morning He had already spent five hours praying to God. Martin Luther King said, "More work gets done through prayer than through work itself."

Hours spent with God make the time we spend with people more effective.

Thus, we can conclude that if we spend hours with God, then it will only take minutes for us to solve any problem here on earth.

The time we spend with God is not wasted; it is invested. Jesus' first priority was not in ministering to men, but to God.

What is needed for God to do His will on earth?

1. **A man or woman that is available.**

"[8]Also I heard the voice of the Lord, saying: "Whom shall I send, and who will go for us?" Then I said, "Here am I! Send me." Isaiah 6.8

God is not interested in our abilities, intellect, capacities, gifts or talents, but in our availability. God is interested in the person who says, "Lord, I give you permission to use my physical body to pray for the lost souls, for the finances, for the government or for the pastor." God wants someone who is willing to pray God's will and to make it happen. God wants to demonstrate His character through our close relationship with Him. God wants us to take dominion and lordship of all that He created. To do this, we must use our physical body and our free will, thus giving Him legal rights to fulfill His purpose and plans on earth.

3

What is Prayer and Why do We Need to Pray?

In my daily walk with God, I have read many books on the subject of prayer. Some of these books were very good; others were filled with concepts and ideas that are contrary to the true meaning of prayer. Before I can teach you what prayer is, I must first define what prayer is not.

Prayer is not…

Prayer is not a monologue or a vain repetition of words: this type of "prayer" is nothing more than worthless chatter. Prayer is not something we do to fulfill some type of quota with God nor is it a religious exercise. Prayer is not asking God for favor, or a way to escape a guilty conscience. Prayer is not like a 911 call that we might make when our lives are on fire and are in need of a "fireman" to extinguish the flames or to help us in our hour of need.

In Matthew 6.7 it says, *"7And when you pray, do not use vain repetitions…"* This verse is clear as to what Jesus thinks about vain repetition.

The more we learn about what prayer is not, the clearer it becomes that we have been practicing vain repetition for a long time. We have not chosen to pray in line with God's heart or His Word. We have had a great deal of conversations or monologues with ourselves. Therefore, we have not been able to see any positive results to our prayers. Now that we understand this concept, we should meditate on the following:

Does God pay attention to this type of skepticism? On one occasion, a man of God was talking to Him concerning vain repetition, how it is done and the fact that this is a prayer of doubt. This man asked God, "What do you do with this type of prayer?" God answered, "I have no idea what you are asking me." In other words, the Lord was saying that He does not hear this type of prayer because it is vain repetition. Many of us have wasted our breath in doing this type of prayer, and because of this, God can't hear us, and because He can't hear us, He can't answer us. With this in mind, we will now learn what prayer really means and the reason why we should do it continually without giving up.

What is prayer?

Prayer is a conversation or a dialogue between our spirit and God. It is the direct communication between our spirit and the Heavenly Father. The reason that I emphasize on the fact that it is between our spirit and God is because God is Spirit, and we talk and pray to Him with our spirit.

"23 But the hour is coming, and now is, when the true worshipers will worship the Father in spirit and truth; for the Father is seeking such to worship Him. 24 God is Spirit, and those who worship Him must worship in spirit and truth." John 4.23, 24

Although the main reason why we have a close relationship with the Father is to have communion with Him, prayer also has other facets with which we can make different types of prayer. For instance, prayer can be used to intercede for others through spiritual warfare, and so on. Before we dig deeper into the need for prayer, we need to analyze a few important aspects about prayer.

Why is it difficult for believers to pray?

This is a very popular question among believers throughout the world. Prayer is a spiritual exercise that is hard to accomplish because it implies that we must be disciplined in that area before we can achieve positive results. There are several reasons why believers have a hard time establishing the daily habit of prayer that is continuous and persevering. Let us go to the book of Matthew and meditate on Jesus' words.

1. **The flesh is weak.**

   "[41] Watch and pray, lest you enter into temptation. The spirit indeed is willing, but the flesh is weak." Matthew 26.41

   All of us need to understand that our flesh is weak. The old man and the old nature, that which we used to be, does not enjoy prayer. Our body is always tired, it wants to sleep longer, it refuses to wake up early and it is always finding ways to excuse the fact that it does not want to pray. If we understand this principle from the beginning, we can do something about crucifying the flesh and putting it under submission. In my own life, I have experienced moments in which my flesh would say, "Sleep another hour." My alarm goes off and my body does not want to get up, but that is when discipline takes over. And so, I get up out of bed, I wash my face and I begin to pray. One reason why this happens is because the flesh is weak and it never wants to surrender a moment of its time to prayer.

2. **The results are never equivalent to the time we invest in prayer.** For some time, many of us have been praying for the same things without ceasing and without any evidence

that our prayers have been heard. When we see no results to our prayers, we give up and stop praying.

3. **Prayer is an investment.** Sometimes we have to invest a lot of our time in prayer in order to see great results. Do not expect to receive great rewards instantaneously when we only invest a few minutes in prayer. To receive answers to our needs, we must invest a lot of our time in prayer and we must do it continually until we obtain the victory.

4. **Because we have no idea how to pray for long periods of time.** One reason why many people find it difficult to pray is because after five or ten minutes they run out of words to say. They are at a loss as to what to say next, and instead of persevering in prayer, they give up, feeling frustrated.

5. **We lack understanding on the subject of prayer.** There is lack of understanding on how to ask God for something, what to do when God speaks to us and how to pray in line with God's Word. Also, not knowing how to pray in the spirit and a total lack of understanding as to the meaning of prayer can frustrate us, leaving us with the final outcome, which is to give up our desire to pray.

What is the proper physical posture for prayer?

The Word of God does not command us to assume a specific physical position that we should pray in, although the Scriptures do mention different physical positions which we can assume during a determined period of time, such as: on our knees, standing, sitting, laying prostrate before His presence, and others. The thing that makes prayer effective is not the physical position that we assume while in prayer, but it is our heart-felt attitude towards God. We should always have a joyful attitude, a holy reverence, and an attitude of thanksgiving and faith. Throughout this book, we will learn answers to the many questions that people are asking themselves concerning prayer. Many people talk about, and write about, prayer, but only a few practice what they preach. A survey was held in which three thousand leaders within the United States, including Pastors, Evangelists, Apostles and Prophets were asked about their personal prayer time and how much time they actually invested in prayer. To everyone's surprise, the survey demonstrated that seventy percent prayed for only thirty minutes a day or less; twenty percent prayed approximately forty five minutes or less; and ten percent prayed at least an hour daily.

If the spiritual condition of our leadership is weak and feeble, then the spiritual condition of those under our responsibility is worse than ours. I strongly believe that the time has come to pray endlessly, to seek His face wholeheartedly, and to stop talking about prayer and actually put it into practice.

Why is prayer a necessity?

"1Then He spoke a parable to them, that men always ought to pray and not lose heart." Luke 18.1

I believe that before I can give an answer to this question, we must ask ourselves other questions regarding certain biblical truths. Later, I will explain why prayer is necessary.

Why should we pray if God is sovereign over all things and He does whatever He wants to do and wherever He wants to do it?

If the Word declares that before we open our mouths, God has already heard our needs, then why should we pray? If Satan and his followers have already been defeated, and Jesus has authority, then why should we pray against the enemy? Why do we have to carry the burden for others if God has done everything that needs to be done? Why should I pray? If the Word of God establishes that it is His will that all men be saved, then, why do we have to pray for the lost souls? The answers to all of these questions can be found in Scripture. We will now answer all of these questions in the clearest and simplest way possible. To begin with, there are many biblical reasons why God wants us to invest time in prayer. Another way to say this is: there are various reasons that explain the need for prayer, such as:

1. **God operates through human beings**

Let us go back for a moment and take a look at how it was at the beginning of creation. God created man and called him Adam, which means "humanity", a human being, a man made of flesh and bones and the one to whom God gave total dominion and lordship over His creation. God wants His perfect will to be done through humanity.

"26Then God said, "Let Us make man in Our image, according to Our likeness; let them have dominion over the fish of the sea, over the birds of the air, and over the cattle, over all the earth and over every creeping thing that creeps on the earth." Genesis 1.26

Man is the administrator or God's representative on earth. Therefore, he is responsible to execute God's dominion and authority; God uses man to do His job. Don't lose sight of the fact that God can do anything, in heaven and on earth, without anyone's help, but it pleases Him to use man, with his imperfection, flaws and weaknesses. God knows that man will inevitably make mistakes, but He still works out His plans and purpose through the prayer of the righteous in Christ.

"7Surely the Lord GOD does nothing, unless He reveals His secret to His servants the prophets." Amos 3.7

The same way we observe how God worked together with Adam, we see Him working through the prophets today. This is one good reason why He needs us to pray. He has chosen us to be co-laborers together with Him in the work that He is doing on earth. God needs human hands to deliver healing, human mouths to speak His words, human feet to travel throughout the nations and to be His representatives. God needs His children to pray and to intercede, thus making it possible for Him to fulfill His plans and purpose.

There are many plans and projects of God that have yet to be fulfilled because there is a shortage of men and women who are willing to give birth to these in the spirit.

2. **God is looking for a family with which to enjoy a close relationship**

One of the many reasons why we need to pray is because God wants to have a family with whom He can enjoy a close relationship. He wants children with whom He can relate and have intimacy with. He wants to talk to them, walk with them, and develop closeness with them, as we learned in the beginning of the book.

"14The secret of the LORD is with those who fear Him, and He will show them His covenant." Psalms 25.14

3. For God's will to be done on earth

"[2]Your will be done on earth as it is in heaven." Luke 11.2

Through prayer, God has fulfilled His will on earth; for everything that has already been done, first, someone had to ask God for it. For example: God has established that it is His will that all men be saved. Therefore, to establish God's will on earth, as it is in heaven, it is necessary for His will to be done through our family. How can this be done? His will is done through prayer. It is imperative for us to remember that when Jesus spoke about prayer He was referring to it as a necessity. A need is something basic and essential for survival. For instance, eating and sleeping are essential to our body as prayer is to our spirit. We need it to survive; otherwise, we are in risk of spiritual death. There are many plans and purposes of God that have yet to be accomplished because God has not found a man or woman willing to pray in line with His will. God is searching the land for willing vessels to proclaim and to declare His Word.

4. Prayer gives God legal rights to change the will of man

It is through prayer that God can deal with, and change, a person who does not want to change his own condition. When prayers are lifted for that particular person, God begins to touch and stir that person, even when this person refuses to change. God is not violating the individual's free will nor his right to choose, neither is He forcing this person to do something against his will. The way that God will touch this stubborn, hardheaded person who refuses to change is by infusing him with the desire to will and to do; this was something that was not there before. Usually, after someone prays, that particular person begins to have a desire to change. Only God can do this through the prayer of a righteous man or woman.

"[13]for it is God who works in you both to will and to do for His good pleasure." Philippians 2.13

The verse that you just read is wonderful! It teaches us that when a person does not want to change, or does not have the desire to change, God places in him not only the desire in his heart, but also the will to see it through. Our prayers can bring about radical changes in humanity, cities and nations. For this reason, prayer is extremely necessary. Perhaps your spouse is set against having a relationship with God, but through your constant prayer, God will place the desire in his heart to know Him and to establish a relationship with Him. Do not stop praying until you see the answer to your prayer. Perhaps, you are also experiencing the lack of desire to fulfill His calling in your life, but you have the desire to pray. If this is your situation, then begin to pray today and He will fill you with the desire and the ability to fulfill His calling in you.

Illustration: "Take the horse for a ride"

Once, there was a life insurance salesman who went to speak with his employer. He was very upset. He said to his boss, "I couldn't sell anything. None of the people that I visited wanted to buy any insurance. And, if you really think about it, I can't force them to buy anything." His boss answered, "You can take a horse to water, but you can't make him drink. However, you can take him for a long ride until he gets thirsty enough, then he will be the one to look for water himself." This is the same thing that happens to those people who do not know the Lord or refuse to do His will.

We can't force them to seek God, but we can pray for them to receive the desire to do it. That is to say, we can take them for a long spiritual run through prayer. Sooner or later, they will be thirsty enough to look for the rivers of living water.

Things are birthed through prayer.

Let us analyze, for just a moment, what happened with Elijah. God tells him to pray for the rain to stop, and it did; for three and a half years it did not rain. However, at the end of 1 Kings, chapter eighteen, Elijah prayed again and asks God for rain to descend once again.

"1 And it came to pass after many days that the word of the LORD came to Elijah, in the third year, saying, "Go, present yourself to Ahab, and I will send rain on the earth." 1 Kings 18.1

"41 Then Elijah said to Ahab, "Go up, eat and drink; for there is the sound of abundance of rain." 1 Kings 18.41

Elijah goes to the top of Carmel and assumes a very distinct and particular position.

"42 So Ahab went up to eat and drink. And Elijah went up to the top of Carmel; then he bowed down on the ground, and put his face between his knees." 1 Kings 18.42

As we read, we see that the position, which Elijah got into, is one that symbolizes travail through prayer, giving birth to things. Prayer gives birth to things in the physical and spiritual realm. God is saying to us that through prayer, we can give birth to lost souls, lands, resources, finances, ministries, and more.

Why did Elijah pray seven times?

In 1 Kings 18:44 we read, *"it came to pass the seventh time, that he said..."* The number seven is the number of perfection and completeness. This is God's number which symbolizes wholeness, it is finished. In prayer, this symbolizes that we have to pray until the work is done, until there is a breakthrough and until the victory is ours.

After reading these verses, perhaps you are left with this question: "Why is perseverance so important in this type of prayer if what is happening was God's idea, it was done in His time and it was His will?" The reason why we must persevere is because although we understand that it was God's idea and will, and that it was during His predetermined time, we need to learn to pray until the "rain" pours. God wants to use us as His vessels to see His will done. How many of God's promises have not been received because He was unable to find a person willing to stand in the gap for the people? When God inspires us to pray, our attitude should be one of gratitude, we should feel privileged because God is using us as part of His divine plan. There are two types of people that God is looking for. He sought after them in the Old Testament and now, in the New Testament times, He wants to use them as His precious instrument to fulfill His plans.

- **Intercessors**

  "30 So I sought for a man among them who would make a wall, and stand in the gap before Me on behalf of the land, that I should not destroy it; but I found no one." Ezekiel 22.30

  Intercessors are people who are willing to stand in the gap for others, as mediators between God and humanity.

They work together with Jesus, who is the only mediator between God and men. They are an extension of the Ministry of Jesus Christ; they stand in prayer on behalf of humanity. Intercessors prepare the way for God's will to be done on earth.

- **Worshippers**

Worshippers open the door for God's glory to descend. While the intercessors plow the earth, the worshippers make the rain come upon the land.

5. Prayer helps you to resist temptation

One of the many reasons why we need to pray is to resist temptation and to receive the benefit of having self control when it comes to temptation. Many believers are unable to resist temptation because they lack a steady life of prayer. Therefore, when the enemy comes against them, they are beaten and defeated.

"41 Watch and pray, lest you enter into temptation. The spirit indeed is willing, but the flesh is weak." Matthew 26.41

6. Prayer is the means that we use to lay down our burdens before God

"7 casting all your care upon Him, for He cares for you." 1 Peter 5.7

"6 Be anxious for nothing, but in everything by prayer and supplication, with thanksgiving, let your requests be made known to God." Philippians 4.6

God gave us the gift of prayer for us to use it as a way to cast all of our cares, our problems and worries upon Him. Many people carry a heavy load all of the time because their prayer life is practically non-existent, hence they have not laid down their burdens before God.

We have learned that God has chosen humanity to fulfill His will on earth. He is looking for a family with which to have fellowship and a close relationship. It is through prayer that God can change a person; He does this by giving man the desire and the will to change. Another reason why we have to pray is to establish God's will on earth, as it is in heaven. Prayer prevents us from falling into temptation and it gives us strength to resist it. Also, prayer is a way to approach God and to surrender all of our anxieties to Him.

What challenges must we overcome before we can begin to pray?

We need to overcome the challenge of time. We need to motivate and make ourselves available for prayer all of the time. Also, we need to deny the desires of the flesh and we must choose to be an instrument in God's hands in order to fulfill His will. We should consider it a privilege that God chooses us to be part of His divine plan. Everyday is a new opportunity to wake up and say, "Lord, I want to begin to establish my prayer life today, I want to be a part of what you are doing. Do it through me!" Remember that prayer is a necessity, and if it is not practiced, we run the risk of drying up spiritually. Make your decision and begin to pray today!

4

Biblical Principles for Effective Prayer

Sometimes, our prayers are not answered because we are missing an essential biblical foundation regarding how to pray effectively. When we are not clear on what it takes to pray effectively, we end up throwing punches in the air, hoping to hit the bull's eye. This happens when we are ignorant as to how to pray effectively. In this chapter, you will learn a few biblical principles for effective prayer, and when you implement these principles in your prayer life, you will begin to see great results.

1. Pray to the Father in the name of Jesus

This principle involves the Father and the name of Jesus. When our Lord was physically present among us, He taught that every prayer should be directed to the Father in His name, the name of Jesus.

"23 And in that day you will ask Me nothing. Most assuredly, I say to you, whatever you ask the Father in My name He will give you. 24 Until now you have asked nothing in My name. Ask, and you will receive, that your joy may be full." John 16.23, 24

Jesus said that when we pray we should begin by saying, *"Our Father, who art in heaven."* Jesus was teaching us that the number one priority in prayer is to have fellowship with the father.

Who is the Father?

The Father is the first person of the Trinity or Deity. The word "Father" in Greek is *"Pater"*, which means founder, protector, provider, source, progenitor, leader, cultivator, and one who provides nourishment. The Hebrew word for Father is *"Abba"*, which means daddy. This word, when it is spoken, expresses a very profound love and tenderness towards God.

For the Jew, it was an insult to call God "daddy" or to call Him by name. They accused Jesus of being a blasphemer because to them, it was inconceivable for Jesus to mention the name of God with such familiarity. When Jesus came to earth, He provided the way for the reconciliation between God, the Father, and humanity through His sacrifice at the cross. Because of His sacrifice of love, we now have the privilege of calling God: Father, Dad or Daddy. What Jesus was really saying was that if our prayers are directed towards Daddy, then our petition will be answered because we would be approaching Him as legitimate children and not as bastards.

"32He who did not spare His own Son, but delivered Him up for us all, how shall He not with Him also freely give us all things?" Romans 8.32

The reason that Jesus teaches us to pray to the Father in His name is because He is our source, our protector, progenitor, provider, cultivator, defender and our sustainer. We are His children and He is our Daddy. He wants to establish a close relationship with us in which we can approach Him and call Him Daddy. Some people have a hard time establishing an intimate relationship with the Heavenly Father because their earthly fathers were not the perfect role models. Therefore, because of their painful experiences with their earthly father, they think that God is the same as their earthly fathers were. They are greatly mistaken. God is a good God and He wants to have a close relationship with His children.

Why did Jesus say to ask anything of the Father in His name? Throughout Scripture, God introduces himself to His prophets by His given name because for the Hebrews, in the Old Testament, the name represented who the person was and what he had. One such example is found in Moses:

"14 And God said to Moses, 'I AM WHO I AM.' And He said, 'Thus you shall say to the children of Israel, I AM has sent me to you.'" Exodus 3.14

God's name is "I am that I am" which is translated from the Hebrew **"YHVH",** and translated into english from the latin as Jehovah. The meaning of this name is so profound that it is difficult to explain. This name represents all that God is, His glory, power and majesty.

What is the meaning of the name YHVH? It means one who lives, one who has life or exists by His own will. In simpler terms, the meaning of His name is: **"I am that I am, I am whom I will be, I am who was, I am the one who exists and shall exist out of my own will to live."** He is the God who embraces all of the verbal conjugations and the One who holds time in His hands. We could continue to try and explain the meaning of everything that God is with human terminology, but it would be impossible. If we were to give it a modern definition, we could say: "I am God, or the everlasting being and I will reveal myself to those who need me." Every time God appeared before His prophets, He would give His name; immediately His prophets would recognize Him because His name represented everything that He was. God appeared before different prophets, priests and kings, and each time, He gave a different name. There are twelve main revelations of His name with which He revealed Himself to His servants in the Old Testament. He also revealed Himself to the people of Israel, but the following revelations are the most relevant.

As you read, keep in mind that in the Hebrew tradition, the name represents the nature and character of the individual. Our God, and Father Jehovah, revealed Himself through the following revelations of His name **YHVH**:

When God wanted to change a man's destiny and purpose, He would add one of the letters of His name to that of the man's. For instance, Abram (father of a multitude) was changed to Abraham (father of many nations). The name of Sarai, which means manipulator, was changed to Sarah, which means princess. The only thing that God did was add the letter "H" to the original name. This was His way of changing the purpose and destiny of a person. Through his name, God added His nature, character, life and authority. God's name is holy, so much so, that it is precisely because of this degree of holiness that His name cannot be used in vain. This is also the reason why Jesus, when He prayed, said, "Hallowed be thy name." First, He teaches us to pray to the Father in His name. Second, He tells us to sanctify His name before going ahead with the prayer. The Lord's Prayer was written, not as an example of what words to repeat over and over again, but rather, as a model to follow when we pray.

The name of Jesus is exalted

In the New Testament, God deposits His power and authority into one name, and the twelve main revelations of His name, found in the Old Testament, God also placed in one name: **Jesus**.

"9Therefore God also has highly exalted Him and given Him the name which is above every name." Philippians 2.9

"[21] far above all principality and power and might and dominion, and every name that is named, not only in this age but also in that which is to come." Ephesians 1.21

Everything in heaven and on earth has a name, but the name of Jesus is above them all.

What does the name Jesus mean?

Jesus is the Hebrew word **"JESHUA"**, which means Jehovah is salvation. The word salvation, in the New Testament, is the Greek word *"soteria"*, which means salvation, healing, deliverance, protection, prosperity, strength and security. These words represent who He is, the living God who lives in the eternal present, as is His name, "I am that I am."

When we mention the name of Jesus, we are really saying that Jehovah is saving, healing, delivering, protecting, prospering and strengthening. When the name of Jesus is pronounced with faith, it produces power because the fullness of the inheritance now in heaven is under this name. Jesus is, and He has, everything that His name implies that He has. When we pray to the Father, in the name of Jesus, it is as if Jesus Himself was the one praying and asking. This is a powerful reason why we must pray to the Father in the name of Jesus.

The reason why the name of Jesus has so much power and authority is because He is God. All other beings such as Buddha, Mohammed, and others, were only flesh and bone. Jesus is the only one who is one hundred percent God and one hundred percent man. God does not exalt the name of ordinary men, He exalts His own name.

Why did God name His Son, Jesus?

1. **Jesus received His name because He humbled Himself. He took the form of a servant and was obedient unto death.**

"[5]Let this mind be in you which was also in Christ Jesus, [6]who, being in the form of God, did not consider it robbery to be equal with God, [7]but made Himself of no reputation, taking the form of a bondservant, and coming in the likeness of men. [8]And being found in appearance as a man, He humbled Himself and became obedient to the point of death, even the death of the cross." Philippians 2.5-8

2. **Jesus inherited His name.**

"[2]...has in these last days spoken to us by His Son, whom He has appointed heir of all things, through whom also He made the worlds." Hebrews 1.2

God made Jesus heir of all things because of His merit.

3. **Jesus received His name because He was triumphant.**

"[14]having wiped out the handwriting of requirements that was against us, which was contrary to us. And He has taken it out of the way, having nailed it to the cross. [15]Having disarmed principalities and powers, He made a public spectacle of them, triumphing over them in it." Colossians 2.14, 15

God granted authority and power to the name of Jesus because He was triumphant against the kingdom of darkness, against the power of hell and against the sting of death. He also conquered the cross, and three days later, He was raised from the dead victoriously. God did not give authority to Jesus on a whim; He gave Jesus power and authority because the Lord humbled Himself and conquered.

"[18]And Jesus came and spoke to them, saying, "All authority has been given to Me in heaven and on earth." Matthew 28.18

How can we apply the name of Jesus during prayer?

"[13]And whatever you ask in My name, that I will do, that the Father may be glorified in the Son. [14]If you ask anything in My name, I will do it." John 14.13, 14

Every prayer that you lift before the Father, in the name of Jesus, will be answered. When we ask in His name, it is as if Jesus Himself was asking the Father. The amplified Bible says, *"[23]And when that time comes, you will ask nothing of Me [you will need to ask Me no questions]. I assure you, most solemnly I tell you, that My Father will grant you whatever you ask in My Name [as presenting all that I AM]." John 16.23*

Every time the Father answers our prayer, He is presenting what Jesus is, "*presenting all that I AM.*" Jesus becomes everything that we need, at the moment that we need it. Jesus is everything. Jesus guarantees and answers all of our prayers. Therefore, ask, and then ask again, and you will receive the things that you need.

Authority in God's name

- There is salvation in the name of Jesus.

  "[12]Nor is there salvation in any other, for there is no other name under heaven given among men by which we must be saved." Acts 4.12

- There is healing in the name of Jesus.

  "[16]And His name, through faith in His name, has made this man strong, whom you see and know. Yes, the faith which comes through Him has given him this perfect soundness in the presence of you all."
  Acts 3.16

- There is deliverance in the name of Jesus.

  "[17]And these signs will follow those who believe: In My name they will cast out demons; they will speak with new tongues."
  Mark 16.17

Who has legal rights or authority to use the name of Jesus?

- Every born again believer.

  "[12]But as many as received Him, to them He gave the right to become children of God, to those who believe in His name." John 1.12

What is authority?

Authority is the Greek word *"exousia"*, which means legal rights, delegated to exercise dominion and lordship. God has granted every born again believer legal rights, or legal power to exercise authority and power in His name. What is power? It is the divine ability to accomplish anything. We, as believers, have authority and divine power to use the name of Jesus and to accomplish anything that is in line with God's Word. Let us examine what happened to certain unbelievers who tried to use the name of Jesus.

"[13]Then some of the itinerant Jewish exorcists took it upon themselves to call the name of the Lord Jesus over those who had evil spirits, saying, "We

exorcise you by the Jesus whom Paul preaches." [14]Also there were seven sons of Sceva, a Jewish chief priest, who did so. [15]And the evil spirit answered and said, "Jesus I know, and Paul I know; but who are you?" [16]Then the man in whom the evil spirit was leaped on them, overpowered them, and prevailed against them, so that they fled out of that house naked and wounded." Acts 19.13-16

Not only were these individuals not able to use the name of Jesus, because they were not God's children, but the evil spirit that they tried to cast out of the man overpowered them.

The name of Jesus has authority in three places:

"[10]...that at the name of Jesus every knee should bow, of those in heaven, and of those on earth, and of those under the earth." Philippians 2.10

Heaven. There are three levels of heaven. The first level is what we see outside with our physical eyes. The second level is where the stars and planets are found. The third level of heaven is where God lives. The name of Jesus has power and authority in every level of heaven.

Earth. This is the place where we live. The name of Jesus has power and authority over everything that is on it.

Under the earth. Deep within the earth is where we find hell. There is no place in this universe where the name of Jesus does not have power and authority. When we speak the name of Jesus, heaven and its inhabitants obey. The galaxies and planets obey. Hell and its inhabitants, demons and those who died without Christ, must also obey His name. Every tongue shall confess that Jesus Christ is Lord and every knee shall bow at the mention of His name.

Following are a few testimonies that demonstrate the power and authority that is in the name of Jesus:

- A missionary in Mexico was assaulted by a thief who stole everything he was carrying. When the missionary began to walk away, the thief pointed his gun at him threatening to shoot. Immediately, the missionary pointed at the thief and said, "In the name of Jesus, I order you to drop your weapon." Instantly, the man fell to his knees, dropped the gun and received Jesus as Lord. He also received the baptism of the Holy Spirit and returned what he had stolen.

- Smith Wigglesworth raised a man who had been dead for two days. He arrived at the funeral home and God spoke to him saying, "Raise him up and resurrect him." Instantly, he began to pray. He pulled the corpse out of the coffin and ordered him to rise in the name of Jesus, but the corpse just fell to the floor. Again, he lifted up the corpse and held him by the throat while he ordered him to rise up, but again he fell to the floor. He did not give up. He picked up the corpse a third time and leaned him up against the wall and ordered him to rise up. Instantly, life came into the corpse and he began to walk. This is one of many things that can happen when we believe in the name of Jesus.

- Smith Wigglesworth was resting at home, when suddenly he was told that his wife was dead. He immediately asked for her body to be transported back to his house. He locked himself in his office, with her lifeless body, and began to order the spirit of death to let her go in the name of Jesus. Instantly, she opened her eyes and asks her husband why he raised her up from the dead. She said it was her time to go. She lived to tell about her experience.

- A man was eating at home when he suffered a heart attack. He died instantly. When his wife walked through the door and saw what had happened, she started to pray, demanding, in the name of Jesus, for her husband to return to earth. At that moment, the man opened his eyes. Later, the husband recalled the moment when he was traveling to heaven. He said that he heard a resounding voice that said, "I order you, in the name of Jesus, to return to earth." The husband says that at that moment, Jesus looked at him, smiled and said, "You must return to earth because my daughter is exercising faith in my name and I have to honor her." Praise God, there is power and authority in His name!

- In Cuenca, Ecuador, while I was praying for the sick, I spoke to a woman and said, "Get up in the name of Jesus." Suddenly, this woman stood up and started to walk. Jesus healed her instantly.

- In Miami, Florida, during a miracle and healing crusade, I was led by the Holy Spirit to pray for nine people who were sitting in wheel chairs. When I said, "Rise up and walk," seven of the nine people stood up and walked.

- I have been a witness to many miracle healings such as cancer, cysts, arthritis, tumors and the miracle of blind eyes being healed. There is power in the name of Jesus. Your prayer life will change drastically when you begin to exercise your faith in the name of Jesus.

How can you develop your faith in the name of Jesus?

"16 And His name, through faith in His name, has made this man strong, whom you see and know. Yes, the faith which comes through Him has given him this perfect soundness in the presence of you all." Acts 3.16

Every believer has a blank check made out in his name. The only thing left to do before cashing it is to fill out what he needs. Make a list of the things that you desire, and ask the Father, in the name of Jesus, anything that is in line with His Word, and these things shall be done for you.

- While in Honduras, I delivered a message on how the name of Jesus is like a blank check at our disposal. I said that we can ask God for anything that we want, as long as it is in line with His Word, and He will grant that which we asked for. While I was preaching, a lady approached me and said, "I suffer from asthma, arthritis and myopia." I stopped the teaching and prayed for her; she was instantly healed from these three infirmities. After praying for her, she said something that impacted my life. She said, "I knew I had a blank check at my disposal, that is the reason why I wrote everything that I needed on that check and God healed me."

Many people fear that the enemy will hear them confessing their needs. If you ask the Father, in the name of Jesus, your prayer will not be interrupted; it will go directly to heaven. Every time we pray in the name of Jesus, our prayers will be answered. God backs His Word and His name; this is why our prayers are guaranteed. Use this blank check to write all of the things that you want your Father to do for you, and I am sure that He will answer because He validates the name of Jesus.

Let us continue in the study of other biblical principles on how to pray effectively.

2. Be specific when you pray

We have learned that the first principle of effective prayer is to pray to the Father in the name of Jesus. The second principle is to be specific when we pray. One downfall of the believer is that he has not learned to be specific when he prays. God teaches us that we must be specific because it is His desire to please us, even in small details. Now that we understand this concept, the next time we pray, we will be specific in our request, and He will answer accordingly. If you do not follow this principle, you take the risk of doubting that God will answer your prayer, and he who doubts should not expect to receive anything of the Lord. The amplified Bible says:

"6Only it must be in faith that he asks with no wavering (no hesitating, no doubting). For the one who wavers (hesitates, doubts) is like the billowing surge out at sea that is blown hither and thither and tossed by the wind. 7For truly, let not such a person imagine that he will receive anything [he asks for] from the Lord,8[For being as he is] a man of two minds (hesitating, dubious, irresolute), [he is] unstable and unreliable and uncertain about everything [he thinks, feels, decides]." James 1.6-8

My personal testimony on how to be specific when you pray:

Twelve years ago, my wife and I did not own a house, but one night we agreed on the style of house that we both wanted and asked the Lord to give it to us with the following specifications: three bedrooms, two baths, a large patio, it had to be located near the children's school and close to the highway. The purchase price had to be between eighty and one hundred thousand dollars. The last thing that my wife asked was for the house to have a special type of plant that produces a big red flower, and this plant had to be located at the front of the house. After we stood in agreement and prayed for the house, we waited for a year. One day, we received a phone call about a house that was for sale, and I went to see it. God confirmed that this house was the answer to our prayer. To our surprise, the house contained three bedrooms, two baths and a large patio. Also, the house was located near a school and the highway. Not only that, but the purchase price was exactly what we had asked for, and the house had a beautiful plant that produced red flowers. God gave us the house exactly as we asked. God does answer our prayers, but we must first learn to be specific at all times.

Many people ask in prayer, but they ask the wrong way, and, as a result, their prayers are not answered. If you are going to pray for a spouse, you have to be specific as to how you want him or her to be. Do you want him or her to be tall or short, a missionary, a preacher or a musician with a servant's heart? If you are praying for a job, you must let God know what kind of job you want, what you want to do and how much you want to earn. If you are praying for a car, then, specify the model, the year, your budget limitations, the color you want the car to be and anything else that is pertinent to you. Therefore, if you want to see great results in prayer, then be specific when you ask God for what you want.

3. Approach God in faith

One reason why many believers are unable to develop a strong prayer life, without ceasing or discouragement, is because they do not experience any physical manifestations when they pray. It is important to keep in mind that when we pray we will not always have a physical awareness that anything is happening.

Sometimes, we can feel God's presence, but this does not happen all of the time. Then what should we do? We should pray by faith and not by emotions.

"[6]But without faith it is impossible to please Him, for he who comes to God must believe that He is, and that He is a rewarder of those who diligently seek Him." Hebrews 11.6

The end of this verse is an interesting one; it says that God is a rewarder of those who seek Him diligently; seeking God has its own reward. "What is that reward?" The reward is that we will receive what we ask of God in prayer.

At the beginning it says, *"for he who comes to God must believe that He is."* This means that we must believe that God is there for us when we pray, even when we have no awareness of His presence. We must learn to pray by faith and not by emotions.

"Those who earnestly and diligently seek Him." (Amplified Bible). This implies that we have to persevere in prayer. We must be constant, even when nothing substantial happens during our prayer time. The only thing that we have to remember is that He is the one who rewards us, if we seek Him wholeheartedly.

4. Ask the Holy Spirit for help

I personally believe that our prayer life would be empty, mechanical, and without life, if it were not for the help that we receive from the Holy Spirit. It is imperative that we ask the Holy Spirit to help us when we pray; otherwise, we would be praying on our own strength, independent from God.

"26Likewise the Spirit also helps in our weaknesses. For we do not know what we should pray for as we ought, but the Spirit Himself makes intercession for us with groanings which cannot be uttered." Romans 8.26

First, we need to meditate on the following key words: *"Likewise the Spirit."* In the amplified Bible it says, *"the Spirit Himself."* These words imply that if we surrender our will, when we pray, He will take control of our prayer, and thus, our prayer will become effective.

The verse also says, *"The Spirit also helps."* The word "help" in Greek is *"antilambano,"* which means to take the place of, one who takes us by the hand, together with or against someone. This is an indication that the Holy Spirit takes us by the hand and leads us to the Father in the name of Jesus. He takes our place, and when we pray against our enemy, He guides and helps us.

"...the Spirit also helps in our weaknesses." These words are also interesting and worthy to point out because as was previously mentioned, one obstacle that we face, which discourages us from seeking God in prayer, is our weak flesh. We do not want to take time to pray nor do we have the desire to do it. When we feel like this, the Holy Spirit takes over. We need to invite Him into our prayer time and ask for His help. One thing that I do before beginning my personal prayer time is to invite the Comforter to help me to pray. When I do this, my prayers become effective, dynamic and the presence of God fills me.

Why do we have to ask the Holy Spirit to help us?

In **Romans 8.26** it says, *"For we do not know what we should pray for as we ought."* Most of the time, we do not comprehend how to pray or what to pray for. For this reason, it is imperative that we ask the Holy Spirit to help us, because He knows God's will for His children. When we pray in line with His will, we will receive the answer to our prayers.

What should we do before we start praying?

Before we begin to ask God for anything, we need to invite the Holy Spirit to help us to pray and to show us the Father's heart and His will. Also, we need to invite Him to take control of our personal agenda for the day.

5. Pray in line with God's Word

God does not answer our prayers simply because we have a specific need. He answers our petitions when we pray in line with His Word.

"14Now this is the confidence that we have in Him, that if we ask anything according to His will, He hears us." 1 John 5.14

What do the words "*according to His will*" mean? When we pray according to His will, we are asking God for something according to His Word and what it says. When we do this, we are guaranteed to have our prayers answered.

Why does God not answer the prayer of many believers?

"3You ask and do not receive, because you ask amiss, that you may spend it on your pleasures." James 4.3

As this verse says, the reason why God does not answer the prayer of many believers is because they do not know how to ask. In other words, our prayers are not in line with God's Word. Instead, they are according to our own pleasure.

Therefore, it is crucial to change the way that we pray in order to obtain positive results. How do we ask according to His will? First, we must know His Word. We must understand what His promises are for each of our needs. For example, if we need something of a material nature, we need to find a verse or a biblical promise that supports that prayer, and then we ask God for it.

Why do we have to pray according to His will?

- **Because God will only stand by His Word.**

"35Heaven and earth will pass away, but My words will by no means pass away." Matthew 24.35

When we pray in line with His Word, God is obligated to fulfill His promises. This is why we can hold fast to His Word, because it is like a firm anchor to our soul. God is real and truthful to His Word; if we ask in line with His will, He will do for us what we ask of Him.

""12Then the LORD said to me, "You have seen well, for I am ready to perform My word."" Jeremiah 1.12

Sometimes we are quick to believe the word of a mere man. For instance, when we are searching for employment, we fill out the application form and turn it over to the supervisor. This man tells you that you have been hired and to return the following week to begin to work. You leave his office rejoicing because you were hired for the job. You know you will receive $500.00 in wages a week because the supervisor tells you, and you begin to plan how you will spend your check. To plan your spending spree, you did not ask the supervisor how much money was in his bank account nor did you ask to see the money that he had on hand. If so, what are you basing your trust in? You are trusting the word of a man (the supervisor) who told you that you were hired and that you would receive $500.00 a week. Now, I ask you a question: "If you can trust the word of a man made of flesh and bone, with weaknesses and defects, how much more should you trust in God's Word and on His promises? Trust that what He has promised, He will do because He is faithful.

In **Romans 3.4** it says, "*4Certainly not! Indeed, let God be true but every man a liar.*"

"20For all the promises of God in Him are Yes, and in Him Amen, to the glory of God through us." 2 Corinthians 1.20

Another reason we must pray in line with His Word is:

- **God's integrity and reputation.**

  If God does not answer our prayers, His integrity and reputation are at stake. Therefore, He will fulfill everything that He has promised that He will do. The following verses clearly show that God will keep His word:

  "14and they will tell it to the inhabitants of this land. They have heard that You, LORD, are among these people; that You, LORD, are seen face to face and Your cloud stands above them, and You go before them in a pillar of cloud by day and in a pillar of fire by night. 15Now if You kill these people as one man, then the nations which have heard of Your fame will speak, saying, 16'because the LORD was not able to bring this people to the land which He swore to give them, therefore He killed them in the wilderness.'"
  Numbers 14.14-16

We need to learn to pray in line with His Word. God is not moved only by our needs, but also because of His Word. We should find God's promises for us and become familiarized with them.

According to the Word, what steps should we take to pray?

1. **We need to decide what we want from God.** We need to remember what we have already learned: it is necessary to be specific. You cannot be indecisive in what you want from God; you must be sure of what you are about to ask.

2. **Look for a biblical verse that supports your petition.** This is where many believers miss it. They are unable to find the verses that support their requests because they do not study the Word and thus, have difficulty finding them. It is very important that your petitions be based on one or more biblical verses; this will guarantee that you will receive the answer to your prayers.

   I strongly believe that we must have Scripture backing up our prayers or any situation that we face. We have to say what Jesus said, *"It is written."* The Word of God must dwell in abundance in our hearts and must be continually on our lips.

3. **Ask God for the things that you need.** One thing that the Bible is clear about is that we do not receive because we do not know how to ask. We must approach our Father with confidence, knowing that He hears us. Trust Him for the things that you need and remember to be specific. Describe carefully the things that you need or want, and He will give you the desires of your heart.

"[24]Therefore I say to you, whatever things you ask when you pray, believe that you receive them, and you will have them." Mark 11.24

4. **You must believe that you will receive what you are asking for.** When you pray, believe and trust. Feel confident that what you are need, will be granted and given to you. Perhaps, you will not see the answer to your prayer right away, but keep trusting; it will come.

"[24]believe that you receive them, and you will have them." Mark 11.24

What should be your attitude after you pray and believe that you have received what you asked for? I will now share with you a few important suggestions that will help you to hold on to your promise and receive your blessing.

- **Do not doubt.** Do not allow the enemy to contaminate you with thoughts of doubt or disbelief. Hold captive every thought that goes against God's Word and cast it out.

- **Meditate on the promise.** Constantly meditate on God's promises, which you received by faith.

  "[7]If you abide in Me, and My words abide in you, you will ask what you desire, and it shall be done for you." John 15.7

- **Give glory and honor to God, with thanksgiving.** Every time you remember your petition, give God thanks and the glory for the answer.

Remember that the steps that you just learned can be used as often as you need. Do not stop praying, and asking until you see your answer manifested in the physical realm and until victory is yours. To sum it all up, we can say that if we want to pray effectively, we must pray to the Father in the name of Jesus. We must be specific every time we ask for something. In other words, use details whenever possible. Pray in faith, and ask the Holy Spirit to help you pray according to His will and in line with His Word. If we do this, our prayer life will improve.

5

How to Develop a Life of Constant Prayer

Another great problem among believers, in the area of prayer, is that they give up waiting for the answers to their prayers too quickly, and thus, they quit persevering. They never see their prayers answered because they simply give up. They are unable to pray continuously. In this chapter, you will learn a few very important points about prayer that will help you to achieve a constant and continuous prayer life.

1. Commitment

What is commitment?

Commitment means to make a quality decision, to hold fast to that decision for a long period of time, and to do it wholeheartedly without looking back.

Commitment is the first step needed to achieve a constant and continuous prayer life. We have to make the decision to pray every day knowing that if we don't, God's will and purpose might not be done in our lives and God will be unable to have a close relationship with us. However, if we pray, He can reveal His purpose, because He uses humanity to fulfill His will. God wants to change and touch the lives of people, nations and continents, and to give them the desire to want and to do. Before any of these things can be accomplished, we must establish a continuous prayer life. Also, if we don't pray, we are in danger of being the victims of temptation. That is why we must make the decision and commit to daily prayer.

What should we do with people who are indecisive and uncommitted to prayer?

"[14]Multitudes, multitudes in the valley of decision! For the day of the LORD is near in the valley of decision." Joel 3.14

Our mission as ministers is to encourage people to make a quality decision, and to develop a daily prayer habit in which they can approach God and seek His face. In the family, the first to lead by example should be the husband, followed by his wife and children.

There are four ways that men can use to bring God's glory and blessings into their homes or over a certain situation:

- **Be the first one to serve.** When men lead the service to God, the blessings will increase in their lives.
- **Be the first one to praise and worship.** Men should be the first to raise their hands in worship as they give honor and glory to God.
- **Be the first one to pray.** When men take the initiative to pray and to seek God's presence, the blessings will increase in their homes. Men have a level of authority that women do not have; it is the authority that they have as high priests, which loosens the priestly blessing upon the family.
- **Be the first one to give tithes.** When men take the initiative to tithe and give offerings, the windows of heaven are opened, and blessings are poured upon the finances in

the home. Every man, as head of the household, must make the commitment to pray without ceasing.

2. Discipline

What is discipline? Discipline means to submit our flesh into servitude in order to achieve a goal. Discipline is not the goal, but the means to get there. In this case, the goal is to pray without ceasing and to persevere in prayer. You cannot rejoice because of your discipline, but you should rejoice in your relationship with God. Discipline is the means that we use when we make the commitment to have a prayer life that is constant and to establish a relationship with God. When we place discipline as a priority in our lives, it will help us to develop self-control.

How did Paul discipline himself?

"27But I discipline my body and bring it into subjection, lest, when I have preached to others, I myself should become disqualified."
1 Corinthians 9.27

The flesh never wants to pray; it is weak and doesn't feel the need or desire to pray, but we must make the decision and commitment to pray every day. Discipline helps us to submit our flesh to God's will. Submit your flesh!

3. Perseverance

Perseverance is the Greek word *"proskarteresis"*, which means to insist; to be strong until; to persevere; to remain steadfast; to stay in one place instead of abandoning it; to have consistency or to be consistent with a person or thing.

"[14]These all continued with one accord in prayer and supplication, with the women and Mary the mother of Jesus, and with His brothers." *Acts 1.14*

"[12]...rejoicing in hope, patient in tribulation, continuing steadfastly in prayer." *Romans 12.12*

"[18]...praying always with all prayer and supplication in the Spirit, being watchful to this end with all perseverance and supplication for all the saints." *Ephesians 6.18*

There are three great enemies of every believer:

Pride. This sin opens the door to every other sin. Lucipher was expulsed from heaven because of his pride.

Fear. This spirit paralyzes you. It is an obstacle that impedes you from being successful (this spirit is also known as fear of success). There are many believers today who are bound by this spirit; they need deliverance.

Lack of perseverance. Pride opens the door to every sin, fear binds and paralyzes, and lack of perseverance immobilizes and detains you from going forth. Lack of perseverance is a great enemy of every believer. You will find people that begin projects, but never finish them. They will begin to serve in a ministry, but quickly abandon it. They begin to change, but give up too quickly. They commit to learning, but give it up before they are finished. They begin to pray on a daily basis, but give up because they lack perseverance. There are many unfinished projects, goals and plans that are the direct result of lack of perseverance. Inconsistency is an evil deed.

The Word of God teaches that we should persevere in prayer, doctrine, salvation, and grace, in fulfilling the Word and in doing what is right.

We often give up on prayer. We start out with enthusiasm for a time, but later we stop or slow down causing our spiritual life to dry up.

What did Jesus say about perseverance and consistency?

"1Then He spoke a parable to them, that men always ought to pray and not lose heart." Luke 18.1

Jesus emphasized two very important points:

1. **Prayer is a necessity.** We need to pray because we have to have communion with God; we are called to do it. God wants to establish His will on earth and to change the will of men. He wants the legal right to work in the heart of men. Also, we need to be constantly reminded that prayer is essential to help us from falling into temptation. Jesus declared that prayer is a necessity.

2. **Pray without ceasing and don't lose heart.** The words "*lose heart*" mean to "fail wholeheartedly", to lose your courage and to want to give up. Jesus said that prayer was a necessity and that it should be practiced daily. This is an important point to remember because many give up too soon.

What else did Jesus say concerning perseverance in prayer?

"7Ask, and it will be given to you; seek, and you will find; knock, and it will be opened to you." Matthew 7.7

The word **"ask"** in Greek is *"aiteo"*, which means to beg; petition or supplication. The word implies to be persistent in asking; to never give up; to never lose heart when the answer is taking too long; and to go forth. Later, Jesus talks about another level of prayer called "seek".

The word **"seek"** implies to seek God with intensity. This is no longer a petition or a supplication; rather, it is an intense and diligent search. It is to search for something until it is found. This word also implies perseverance, but with greater intensity. The last, but not least, level of prayer is to "knock".

The word **"knock"** is also translated as "knocking at the door until it falls." This word implies an intense search **until** there is a breakthrough. This type of search has no limitations. Jesus said to *ask and continue to ask*, but if you don't see any results, *seek* intensely until you find what you are looking for. If nothing happens, then *knock* at the door "until" it falls down. Don't stop praying until you receive the answer. When we go into the last phase, it is no longer a calling, but it is a groaning, moaning or wailing, which will give birth to something in the spirit. We must pray until there is a breakthrough. Paul said:

"19My little children, for whom I labor in birth again until Christ is formed in you." Galatians 4.19

This verse implies that we cannot let the new believers go "until" a change occurs in them.

What does the word "until" mean?

"Until" means a period of time or space; it could be long or short in duration. Sometimes we must pray for some people for long periods of time "until" God finishes what He started in them; as it was in the case of Elijah, who had to pray seven times. The word "until" in Greek means to be attached to a purpose and to not give up. We need to have purpose when we pray, and we should do it until victory is achieved.

Let us examine a few examples of consistency and perseverance that have achieved surprising results.

- Thomas Edison tried out his experiment over 18,000 times before he was successful.

- Albert Einstein tried ninety-nine times to come up with an answer, but it was on the hundredth time that he finally got it; he invented the law of relativity.

- Abraham Lincoln ran for president seven times before he was elected president. He became one of the best presidents that this country has ever had.

- The Israelites had to march seven times around the walls of Jericho before the walls tumbled down and victory was theirs.

- Naaman had to dip in the Jordan River seven times, not six, before he received healing from leprosy. He had to do it "until" he received healing.

Perseverance and consistency implies never to give up, to refuse to lose heart and to remain in one place regardless of the opposition.

- This is what happened to a woman who never gave up praying for her husband. She prayed for 27 years for his salvation. One day, her husband suffered a heart attack and

> died, but she didn't give up. She said, "he can't die, I have prayed for over 27 years for his salvation and he has not received it yet, therefore he can't die." She took her husband's body and locked herself with it and began to pray, asking God to bring him back to life. She prayed for one hour, two hours, six hours, eight hours, and on the fourteenth hour, the man came back to life. He received Jesus as Lord and Savior, became a deacon in the church and lived another ten years. It was a very difficult "until", but this woman saw God's glory manifested in her life because she persevered.

Let us study the life of Jesus for a moment and see how He exalts consistency in perseverance and persistence.

A friend comes at midnight

"5And He said to them, "Which of you shall have a friend, and go to him at midnight and say to him, "Friend, lend me three loaves; 6for a friend of mine has come to me on his journey, and I have nothing to set before him'; 7and he will answer from within and say, "Do not trouble me; the door is now shut, and my children are with me in bed; I cannot rise and give to you'? 8I say to you, though he will not rise and give to him because he is his friend, yet because of his persistence he will rise and give him as many as he needs. 9So I say to you, ask, and it will be given to you; seek, and you will find; knock, and it will be opened to you. 10For everyone who asks receives, and he who seeks finds, and to him who knocks it will be opened. 11If a son asks for bread from any father among you, will he give him a stone? Or if he asks for a fish, will he give him a serpent instead of a fish? 12Or if he asks for an egg, will he offer him a scorpion? 13If you then, being evil, know how to give good gifts to your children, how much more will your heavenly Father give the Holy Spirit to those who ask Him!" Luke 11.5-13

In meditating on these verses, we can make the following observations:

In Luke 11.8 it says, ***"yet because of his persistence he will rise and give him as many as he needs."*** The word "persistence" in this verse means shameful insistence, to claim one's petition until it reaches the limit and to be unashamed to ask. What is Jesus trying to tell us through this verse? Jesus is saying that perseverance is the key to getting answers to our prayers. We cannot give up too quickly. We must continue knocking on the door even when the circumstances seem difficult and opposing. Continue to pray and take your petition to the limit until you obtain the victory. You should not feel shame to ask. Continue asking until you are victorious in your home, health and anything else you might be asking God for.

The Parable of the Persistent Widow

"1Then He spoke a parable to them, that men always ought to pray and not lose heart, 2saying: "There was in a certain city a judge who did not fear God nor regard man. 3Now there was a widow in that city; and she came to him, saying, "Get justice for me from my adversary.' 4And he would not for a while; but afterward he said within himself, "Though I do not fear God nor regard man, 5yet because this widow troubles me I will avenge her, lest by her continual coming she weary me."' 6Then the Lord said, "Hear what the unjust judge said. 7And shall God not avenge His own elect who cry out day and night to Him, though He bears long with them? 8I tell you that He will avenge them speedily. Nevertheless, when the Son of Man comes, will He really find faith on the earth?" Luke 18.1-8

Let us study in depth the previous verses and meditate on a few key words.

In Luke 18.2 it says,*" There was in a certain city a judge who did not fear God nor regard man."* These words refer to the judges of His time who were Jews and who worked for the Roman Empire. They were corrupt judges, traitors to their people and hired by the Roman government to do their biting.

In Luke 18.3 it says, *"[3]Now there was a widow in that city."* During those days, widows did not have any covering or male protection. They were exposed to the abuse of the people, many of whom took advantage of them because they were alone, without friends or family, without protection and without a lawyer who would stand on their behalf and defend them. They were poor and the possibility of winning a case before the judge was practically non-existent. This widow met all of these characteristics, but she had something others did not have. She had something that gave her the victory.

In Luke 18.5, it says, *"[5]yet because this widow troubles me I will avenge her, lest by her continual coming she weary me."* This widow was persistent. She continually went before the judge asking him for justice. This expression: "avenge me" implies to protect, defend and make justice. This woman never gave up, so much so, that the corrupt judge said, "if I don't defend her, if I don't protect her, if I don't give her what belongs to her, she is going to cause great trouble for me, she is going to wear me out. Her perseverance is going to drive me crazy! I don't fear God or man, but her perseverance and her continuous showing up at my office, forces me to defend, protect and to give her what belongs to her."

Later on, Jesus said, *"Hear what the unjust judge said."* In other words, the Lord said that her perseverance was what granted her victory. She knocked on the door, once, twice, three times, and it did not open, but finally, she received what she was asking for. Sometimes, when we knock at the door once and it does not open, we give up, but I encourage you to continue praying and knocking. God will give you the victory. If a door is closed at work, at home or in the family, don't give up, keep knocking!

Now, the Lord cleared something up when He said, ***"7And shall God not avenge His own elect who cry out day and night to Him, though He bears long with them? 8I tell you that He will avenge them speedily. Nevertheless, when the Son of Man comes, will He really find faith on the earth?"*** Jesus said that if the corrupt judge, the one who does not fear God and who sold himself for money was able to provide justice to the persistent widow, who did not have any financial support or defender on her behalf, how much more will our Heavenly Father, the Righteous Judge of the Universe, provide justice for us! How much more will our Father protect, defend and give us what belongs to us if we persevere and call out to Him day and night. We have a defender who stands for us and protects us in the Heavenly Court. If you have been praying for your family's salvation, for healing, for your marriage, and you have not seen any results, continue knocking on the door because your persistence will give you the breakthrough that you are looking for. Persevere and do not give up!

How do we know when we have a breakthrough?

Some people tell me, "Pastor, I am tired of praying." Or they ask me, "How do I know when I should stop praying or to continue?" Sometimes, when we pray for something for a long time, the burden begins to feel heavier than usual, perhaps even get worse. This is a sure sign that the miracle is near. We must never give up, even when we think nothing is happening, instead, we should intensify our prayer time. When we do this, we will begin to identify the signs that a breakthrough is near and we will know for certain that the victory is ours. Now the only thing to wait for is the physical manifestation of the miracle.

Now we will learn a few of the signs that we should be aware of when our breakthrough is evident.

1. **A new song in the spirit.** When you are praying for something specific and suddenly a new song comes into your heart, this is a sign that you have the breakthrough that you were waiting for.

2. **A smile in the spirit.** Some people experience the urge to joyfully smile when they are praying; perhaps they might even begin to laugh without understanding why. This is a sign that God has heard your prayer and that the only thing left to do is to wait for it to manifest in the natural.

3. **Inner peace.** When you are praying for something and suddenly a calming peace comes upon you, this means that you have reached your "until" moment of prayer; you have your breakthrough.

4. **The inner witness.** Sometimes God speaks to us, letting us know that He is in control. Once we hear from God the only thing left to do is to wait until we have the physical manifestation of that which we have been asking for. After we receive the breakthrough we were waiting for, we should begin to give thanks to God for the answer and for the victory.

Following is an example on how to pray until there is a breakthrough:

Several years ago, I was burdened by the Lord to pray for my family. At the time, only one of my brothers was saved and the Lord put it in my heart to pray for the rest of my family. I prayed the same thing over and over again for several days. For three days, I fasted and prayed. I began to pray intensely for them, so much so, that I literally felt like I was giving birth. After three hours of intense intercession, I began to groan and moan in the spirit, followed by a new song that came from deep within me, and I also began to laugh. Immediately, I heard the voice of God that said, "Your family is under my control, they will all be saved." Shortly after that, one by one, each of my brothers received the Lord. Six months later, they were all saved. The breakthrough came and the manifestation of it was evident. It took many days, but the victory was mine. My advice to you is that if you are praying for something for a long time and you have yet to see the breakthrough, then continue to pray and intercede. Do not give up. Do not surrender. God will give you the victory.

Obstacles that will stand in the way of a breakthrough:

- Not seeing any change in the people, things or situation for which we are praying.

- When the outcome of our prayer is not in line with the time that we invested.

- The false reports or well-intentioned words of advice from the brothers or sisters in the faith will sometimes become words of discouragement.

- Distraction during prayer.

In conclusion, prayer must be a lifestyle choice that requires discipline, commitmet and perseverance.

How should we begin?

The first thing we need to do is to make the commitment to pray every day. Regardless of what is happening around us, it is important to keep our commitment to pray and to maintain a close relationship with God. A decision that is not accompanied by discipline will never work. We must begin to submit our flesh and to discipline ourselves in prayer. Many believers purpose in their hearts to pray, but because they never discipline themselves to do it, they lack perseverance and soon give it up. It is necessary to persevere wholeheartedly, asking the Holy Spirit to help you in your weaknesses and to persevere.

6

Prayer Obstacles

During the years that I have ministered the Word of God, I have seen the frustration in God's people. The reason they are frustrated is because their prayers are not being answered; they pray endlessly without a breakthrough. We need to remember that the Lord delights in answering the prayers of His people. His Word teaches that if we ask according to His will, then He hears and answers. If our prayers are not being answered in the way that we expect, then we must ask the Holy Spirit to help us find out what the problem is and what is blocking the answer to our prayer. In this chapter, we will learn what prevents our prayers from being answered.

1. You do not ask or you ask for the wrong thing

The Word of God says:

"2...you do not have because you do not ask. 3You ask and do not receive, because you ask amiss, that you may spend it on your pleasures." James 4.2-3

Many people think that God is too busy to hear us. Others believe that their petitions and needs are too insignificant for God to pay any attention because small matters do not interest Him. Some people believe that the things that they are asking God are too big for God to answer them. But God's Word says that we don't receive because we do not ask. It is because of His Word that I encourage you today to ask God because He wants to grant you the desires of your heart. If you do not receive anything, it is because you are not asking in line with His Word, not because they are too big or insignificant. God wants to bless you. *"[3]You ask and do not receive, because you ask amiss, that you may spend it on your pleasures."*

Other instances are quite the opposite. Some people ask God for things that seem to be in line with His Word, but the intention of their heart is to satisfy some fleshly desire. Their selfish desires or intentions are for self-gratification and not to build up the kingdom of heaven or to bless others. What is worse, their petitions are intended to please and satisfy personal carnal desires such as jealousy, personal glory and satisfaction, competition, and envy, among many. Their motivation is wrong. What should we do? We should continue to ask God for the things that we need or want, but we should do it with the right intention and motivation; this will be evident when we ask. First, we should ask to establish kingdom blessings, then for your family and then for yourself. If you follow this order, then you have overcome the first obstacle that hinders your prayer from being answered.

2. Spousal abuse

"[1]Wives, likewise, be submissive to your own husbands, that even if some do not obey the word, they, without a word, may be won by the conduct of their wives." 1 Peter 3.1

"[7]Husbands, likewise, dwell with them with understanding, giving honor to the *wife, as to the weaker vessel, and as being heirs together of the grace of life, that your prayers may not be hindered." 1 Peter 3.7*

The Apostle Paul teaches what the roles and functions of the man and woman are in the home. He said that women should submit to their husbands, and if she does not, it is considered a form of rebellion against God. Paul tells the husbands to treat their wives as weaker vessels. If the husband mistreats his wife and refuses to love her as she needs to be loved, and perhaps go as far as to physically, verbally or emotionally abuse her, it is considered a form of disobedience to God and His Word. Also, if this behavior is evident in the wife, as well as in the husband, their prayers will be considered a stench and will not be heard. Spousal abuse is a prayer obstacle. When we change the way that we treat our spouse and our attitude towards them also changes, we begin to see a positive return on the time that we invest in prayer. Husbands, do you want your prayers to be answered? Then begin to treat your wives with tender, loving care, and wives, if you want your prayers answered, begin to submit to your husbands.

3. Skepticism or doubt

The word **"doubt"** in Greek is *"aporeo"*, which means to be without direction, without resources, in a bind, perplexed, in doubt, confused, in hopelessness, anxious and unsteady regarding the path that one should take. One thing that God teaches us is that doubt kills and destroys all hope of ever receiving anything from Him. To doubt is a terrible thing. It causes confusion and hesitation. Confusion is the result of a person who doubts. Let us analyze some of the words that describe *"aporeo"* or doubt:

- **Without direction.** This means to be insecure as to where we are going, or which way to take when we are faced with various alternatives.

- **Without resources.** A person who doubts will feel that he or she does not have the necessary resources to finish what he or she started.

- **Perplexed.** A person who finds himself in a state of "shock" has no idea which way to turn.

- **Confused.** A confused person has many thoughts and is unable to make the right decision because he or she is unclear as to what to do.

- **Hesitate.** This word represents the worst aspect of doubt. The miracle is near, it arrives, but because of a hesitant attitude, he or she is unable to receive the answer to prayer because they begin to wonder if perhaps it could be something else instead.

What should we understand about the meaning of the word "doubt"?

We cannot pray and ask God for anything, if we are in doubt of His existence. If we are anxious or confused about what we are asking, then we won't be able to pray with confidence. If we are perplexed, we won't be able to pray with power. If we hesitate concerning His will, we won't be able to obtain the results that we expect. We must change our attitude and begin to believe God and His Word without doubt.

"28And Peter answered Him and said, "Lord, if it is You, command me to come to You on the water." 29So He said, "Come." And when Peter had come down out of the boat, he walked on the water to go to Jesus. 30But when he saw that the wind was boisterous, he was afraid; and beginning to sink he cried out, saying, "Lord, save me!" 31And immediately Jesus stretched out His hand and caught him, and said to him, "O you of little faith, why did you doubt?" Matthew 14.28-31

In the verses that you just read, we see what happened to Peter when he doubted the words of Jesus, he began to sink. This is the same that happens to us today. We see many believers overwhelmed by crisis in their lives because there is doubt in their hearts. If you are in doubt, then none of your petitions will be answered. When does doubt enter our hearts? When we fix our eyes on the circumstances around us instead of on Jesus. "30*But when he saw that the wind was boisterous, he was afraid.*" When we doubt, faith leaves and fear strolls right in. When we fall prey to fear, we immediately begin to drown in our sorrows. Doubt is nothing more than believing what the enemy can do against us.

Sometimes, doubt comes in the form of a thought. The enemy will send a thought that is contrary to what you believe. His purpose in doing this it to divide your thoughts and make you focus on only his negative thought. Once he is successful in making you doubt God's promises, you will begin to go back and forth between God's Word and the devil's negative thoughts. God's only desire is for you to focus on Him and His Word. The devil's plan is to play with your mind.

What should we do when doubt comes into our minds? We have to take it captive to the obedience in Christ. We can't waver between two thoughts. We can't go from healing to sickness in one breath. We must believe that by His stripes we are healed. Never give attention to thoughts of sickness, rather, rebuke them and cast them out.

"4*For the weapons of our warfare are not carnal but mighty in God for pulling down* strongholds." *2 Corinthians 10.4*

What is the answer to doubt?

We must hear and meditate on God's Word. We must continuously think on God's promises found in the Bible and base our prayers in line with these promises. We need to saturate our home, our car, and every where we go with God's Word. The answer to doubt is to learn what the Word of God says, and when we stop doubting, our prayers will be answered.

4. Unforgiveness

Unforgiveness is one of the greatest obstacles to our prayers. Many believers are frustrated and discouraged. They are living in a state of spiritual poverty, unable to walk with their heads held high. Because of this defeated attitude, the breakthrough to their prayers is far from them. One reason for the delay is the unforgiveness that they harbor in their hearts. Many try to masquerade their unforgiveness with statements such as: "I was offended." "I only feel resentment towards him or her." "I am only angry or bothered." "I have something against that person." "I feel hurt." These to mention only a few, but the Word of God is clear on this matter:

"25 And whenever you stand praying, if you have anything against anyone, forgive him, that your Father in heaven may also forgive you your trespasses." Mark 11.25

What did Jesus say about being angry with our brother?

"22 But I say to you that whoever is angry with his brother without a cause shall be in danger of the judgment. And whoever says to his brother, "Raca!" shall be in danger of the council. But whoever says, "You fool!" shall be in danger of hell fire." Matthew 5.22

The amplified Bible says, *"22 But I say to you that everyone who continues to be angry with his brother or harbors malice (enmity of heart) against him shall be liable to and unable to escape the punishment imposed by the court; and whoever speaks contemptuously and insultingly to his brother shall be liable to and unable to escape the punishment imposed by the Sanhedrin, and whoever says, You cursed fool! [You empty-headed idiot!] shall be liable to and unable to escape the hell (Gehenna) of fire."* Unforgiveness, offenses, hurts, wounds and resentment are the guillotine to our prayers. God places us against the wall and says that if we don't let that hurt go, that malice, offense, wounded feeling or resentment from our hearts, then He is not going to forgive or hear our prayers. Heaven will be like bronze for us. Unforgiveness breaks our relationship with God. He is unable to hear our prayer if we harbor something against our brother.

Why does God not forgive our offenses when we choose not to forgive others? Let us meditate on what Jesus said:

"21Then Peter came to Him and said, "Lord, how often shall my brother sin against me, and I forgive him? Up to seven times?" 22Jesus said to him, "I do not say to you, up to seven times, but up to seventy times seven. 23Therefore the kingdom of heaven is like a certain king who wanted to settle accounts with his servants. 24And when he had begun to settle accounts, one was brought to him who owed ***him ten thousand talents.*** *25But as he was not able to pay, his master commanded that he be sold, with his wife and children and all that he had, and that payment be made. 26The servant therefore fell down before him, saying, "Master, have patience with me, and I will pay you all.' 27Then the master of that servant was moved with compassion, released him, and forgave him the debt. 28"But that servant went out and found one of his fellow servants who owed him* ***a hundred denarii;*** *and he laid hands on him and took him by the throat, saying, "Pay me what you owe!' 29So his fellow servant fell down at his feet and begged him, saying, "Have patience with me, and I will pay you all.' 30And he would not, but went and threw him into prison till he should pay the debt. 31So when his fellow servants saw what had been done, they were very grieved, and came and told their master all that had been done. 32Then his master, after he had called him, said to him, "You wicked servant! I forgave you all that debt because you begged me. 33Should you not also have had compassion on your fellow servant, just as I had pity on you?'*

[34]And his master was angry, and delivered him to the torturers until he should pay all that was due to him. [35]"So My heavenly Father also will do to you if each of you, from his heart, does not forgive his brother his trespasses." Matthew 18.21-35

The verses that you just read give us many important key factors that we need to meditate on.

Notice that a *talent* was a unit of measure used to weigh the gold. A *talent* was equivalent to approximately 75 pounds and 10,000 *talents* were equal to 750,000 pounds or 375 tons. Today, the prize for one ounce of gold is approximately $375.00. Therefore, at today's prices, one pound of gold is worth $6,000.00, a *talent* of gold or 75 pounds is equal to $450,000.00 and 10,000 *talents* of gold are equal to $4,500,000,000.00. In other words, the servant owed his master this incredible amount of money. Jesus was trying to teach us with this passage that the servant had a debt that could never be repaid. We have such a debt that we can not repay, but Jesus cancelled our debt; He canceled the decree that was designed to destroy us.

"[13]And you, being dead in your trespasses and the uncircumcision of your flesh, He has made alive together with Him, having forgiven you all trespasses, [14]having wiped out the handwriting of requirements that was against us, which was contrary to us. And He has taken it out of the way, having nailed it to the cross." Colossians 2.13-14

Going back to the previous Scripture, what was a denarii? It was approximately the salary for one day's work. Today, this is approximately $52.00 per day. If this is true, then 100 denarii are aproximately $5,200.

There is a great amount of difference between $4,500,000,000 that the servant owed the king and $5,200 that the servant owed his master. This is similar to the debt that we had with God; impossible to pay. We had thousands of debts, but God forgave them all. Perhaps someone has offended or mistreated you, but this will never compare to what we have done against God. Thousands of sins against a few offenses are really nothing to speak of. The person who chooses or who feels like he can't forgive has forgotten how many sins Jesus forgave him or her. If we were to consider the age we started to have knowledge or understanding of sin, and how many sins we are guilty of since then, the total sum would be astronomical. Perhaps, if we were to total the number of times that we sinned against God up until now, we could probably come up with 10,000, 15,000, 40,000 or more sins that have been forgiven by Jesus. Taking this into consideration, is it impossible for us to forgive the people that have offended us twenty or thirty times?

What happens when we don't forgive?

In Matthew 18.34,35, the Word tells us that we will be turned over to our torturers; these are demons and the consequences that we must face are poverty, wretchedness, sickness and depression, among too many to mention. When this happens, we have no one to blame but ourselves. Through sin, we give the enemy legal rights to destroy us. This also prevents our prayers from being answered. Anger, resentment, bitterness and hate follow the cycle of unforgiveness. Let us meditate on the following verse:

"[8]*Again, a new commandment I write to you, which thing is true in Him and in you, because the darkness is passing away, and the true light is*
already shining. [9]*He who says he is in the light, and hates his brother, is in*
darkness until now. [10]*He who loves his brother abides in the light, and there*
is no cause for stumbling in him. [11]*But he who hates his brother is in*

darkness and walks in darkness, and does not know where he is going, because the darkness has blinded his eyes." 1 John 2.8-11

"[14]We know that we have passed from death to life, because we love the brethren. He who does not love his brother abides in death. [15]Whoever hates his brother is a murderer, and you know that no murderer has eternal life abiding in him." 1 John 3.14,15

What should we do when someone offends us?

"[26]Be angry, and do not sin, do not let the sun go down on your wrath." Ephesians 4.26

The *amplified* Bible says, *"[26]When angry, do not sin; do not ever let your wrath (your exasperation, your fury or indignation) last until the sun goes down."*

Never leave pending any unresolved issues; otherwise, the offense you don't forgive today will eventually turn into bitterness and hate. If you ever get to the extreme point of loathing someone, you will certainly walk in darkness and desolation. All of your prayers will be rejected. There are many blessings from God that are now on hold because of our unforgiving attitude. The condition of our hearts, what we feel, and how we deal with unresolved offenses, is what stops God's blessings from ever coming, and above all, it is a major obstacle to having our prayers answered.

In closing, the greatest obstacles to our prayer life are: not asking or not knowing how to ask, spousal abuse, doubt and unforgiveness. We need to make every effort to avoid temptation in these areas. If we do this, every prayer will be answered.

7

How to Pray for One Hour Using Different Types of Prayer

One complaint that many believers have is, "I can not pray for long periods of time. I simply run out of things to say. I ask God for the things that I need, and then, I don't know where to go from there." With God's help, I will teach you to pray for one hour or more. You will learn how to pray for longer periods of time, using different kinds of prayers; each prayer has a specific purpose and they are all necessary. In Ephesians 6.18 it says, *"Praying always with all prayer and supplication."*

In this chapter, we will define and study the purpose for each kind of prayer. Also, you will learn how to pray for one hour or more, using twelve kinds of prayers.

I. The praise and worship prayer

This kind of prayer is used to worship God for what He is and for what He does. Every time you decide to pray, you should begin with a time of praise and worship. As soon as you open your mouth, you should begin to exalt God's greatness. Many believers have yet to understand what it means to praise God. Today, I will try to teach you what I know.

What is praise?

Praise means to honor, glorify, admire and celebrate God's **goodness** and wonderful works. Praise is a brilliant, radiant, shining, magnificent and living celebration. The more you exalt and magnify God through praise, the happier you will be and your understanding of Him will intensify and deepen. This genuine expression of praise will lift up your spirit. You will be overwhelmed, to such an extreme, that you will begin to boast and brag about your God. As a result, your praise will make you noisy, loud and outspoken. You will begin to express what He is and who He is. It will seem as if you had lost your mind for an instant. You will begin to resemble a person who is outside of yourself, as if you had too much to drink and simply lost all self-control. You will appear to be delirious or crazy. Some people might even say that you were making a fool of yourself.

The following verses describe David's attitude when he praised God:

"13And *so it was, when those bearing the ark of the* LORD *had gone six paces, that he sacrificed oxen and fatted sheep.* 14*Then David danced before the* LORD *with all his might; and David was wearing a linen ephod.* 15*So David and all the house of Israel brought up the ark of the* LORD *with shouting and with the sound of the trumpet.* 16*Now as the ark of the* LORD *came into the City of David, Michal, Saul's daughter, looked through a window and saw King David leaping and whirling before the* LORD*; and she despised him in her heart.* 20*Then David returned to bless his household. And Michal the daughter of Saul came out to meet David, and said, "How glorious was the king of Israel today, uncovering himself today in the eyes of the maids of his servants, as one of the base fellows shamelessly uncovers himself!"* 21*So David said to Michal, "It was before the* LORD*, who chose me instead of your father and all his house, to appoint me ruler over the people of the* LORD*, over Israel. Therefore I will play music before the* LORD*.* 22*And I will be even more undignified than this, and will be humble in my own sight. But as for the maidservants of whom you have spoken, by them I will be held in honor."*
2 Samuel 6.13-16, 20-22

In the Merriam-Webster dictionary, the word "praise" means to express a favorable judgment of, or to glorify God, especially by the attribution of perfections; to express praise. In simple terms, praise means to give God the honor and the glory through which you express your admiration. Praise changes the priority in your lives, from yourself to God. Praise is a conscious decision; an act of your will.

"15Therefore by Him let us continually offer the sacrifice of praise to God, that is, the fruit of our lips, giving thanks to His name." Hebrews 13.15

A sacrifice of praise is the kind of praise that you give to God out of obedience, regardless of how you feel. The word "sacrifice" in Greek is *"Thuo"*, which means to kill or assassinate with purpose. When you offer a sacrifice of praise to God, what you are really doing is killing your pride, selfishness, self-righteousness, laziness, tiredness and the desires of the flesh. What happened the first time that you raised your arms to the Lord? You felt embarrassed. What happens now when you are going through a crisis? The last thing you want to do is talk about it, much less praise God in the midst of it. Then, what should you do when you do not have the desire to praise or worship God? The answer is easy, begin to offer your sacrifice of praise to God; kill everything that is holding you back from adoring Him.

When should you praise God?

God is worthy of your praise and of your worship all of the time. It does not matter what time of the day it is, you should begin praising Him the moment that you wake up and continue praising Him throughout the day until it is time to sleep again. Begin your prayer praising Him for the things that He has done.

In good times and in bad, when you are out of work, when your bank account is empty, in sickness or in health, in private or in public, praise is the way that you make room for God in your life.

"[1]I will bless the LORD at all times; His praise shall continually be in my mouth." Psalms 34.1

Some principles of praise:

You do not need a special reason to praise Him. Every moment, every instant is the perfect time for praise. At the beginning of each day, praise will give you the strength to overcome any adversity that you might have to face during the course of your day. Your griping and complaining destroys the atmosphere created by praise. How should you praise and worship God? You need to create your own concert instead of settling for attendance only.

Biblical ways on how to praise God:

Singing – This is the most common way to praise God.

"[4]Sing praise to the LORD, you saints of His, and give thanks at the remembrance of His holy name." Psalms 30.4

"[19]...speaking to one another in psalms and hymns and spiritual songs, singing and making melody in your heart to the Lord." Ephesians 5.19

Shouting – This word in Hebrew is *"ranan"*, which means to shout and sing with power. To shout is to let out a gust of wind from your mouth, and if possible, the force of this wind should break stones in half; to rupture the ears with a powerful sound.

An example on how to praise God is by shouting with all of your strength, "You are great!"

Laughing – This is an extremely rare form of praise today. When you experience this form of praise, and begin to laugh, sometimes uncontrollably, people around you will think that what is happening is weird, but believe it or not, this, too, is another way to praise God.

"21 He will yet fill your mouth with laughing, and your lips with rejoicing." Job 8.21

Thanksgiving – When you give thanks to God for everything that He does for you, you are praising Him.

"30 ...to stand every morning to thank and praise the LORD, and likewise at evening." 1 Chronicles 23.30

Bowing down – This is when you get on your knees and bend over as a sign of humbleness before God; this is an act of respect and reverance.

Kneeling down – Kneeling down before your God is an act of humbleness and honor to Him. This is where you recognize that He is God and that you are His child. Sadly, but true, many churches no longer practice this form of praise because it causes people to feel shame.

"6 Oh come, let us worship and bow down; let us kneel before the LORD our Maker." Psalms 95.6

Applauding – Clapping is praise; it demonstrates your appretiation for God. Unfortunately, there are many churches today that forbid people from clapping during a church service or meeting. To applaud means to make noise, not the kind of gentle noise that you would expect in an opera, but the kind of noisy, loud and deafening applaud, like the sound of thunder. This form of praise expresses His greatness when words are not sufficient. In simpler terms, to applaud is "not" to make a delicate sounding noise, like that of an elegant clap heard during an opera, but rather, it is to make a very loud, deafening sound, something that might resemble powerful thunder.

"[1]Oh, clap your hands, all you peoples! Shout to God with the voice of triumph!" Psalms 47.1

Dancing – This form of praise was very common in Bible days. It is the movement of your entire body as you praise God.

"[1]Praise the LORD! Praise God in His sanctuary; Praise Him in His mighty firmament!" Psalms 150.1

In Luke 10.21, it says, *"rejoiced in the Spirit."* The word "rejoice" in Greek means to "jump for joy." This same word in Hebrew means to "turn many times in the air while under the influence of a violent emotion." To "rejoice" means to spin or rotate in the air. This word implies that you don't realize nor are you conscious of what you are doing. How many times does the Lord motivate you to dance in the Spirit and you doubt if you should do it or not because you feel ashamed?

Raising your hands – Some of us, on a rare ocassion, raise our hands to praise God, but He is telling us to do it as an act of praise.

"[4]Thus I will bless You while I live; I will lift up my hands in Your name." Psalms 63.4

Talking and singing in tongues – We praise God when we talk and sing in other tongues or in the Spirit. This is where our spirit speaks directly with God.

"[15]What is the conclusion then? I will pray with the spirit, and I will also pray with the understanding. I will sing with the spirit, and I will also sing with the understanding." 1 Corinthians 14.15

Worshipping Him with music and instruments – This is the most common form of praise; with music, using every kind of instrument available.

"[1]Praise the LORD! Praise God in His sanctuary; Praise Him in His mighty firmament! [2]Praise Him for His mighty acts; Praise Him according to His excellent greatness! [3]Praise Him with the sound of the trumpet; Praise Him with the lute and harp!" Psalms 150.1-3

Why should you praise Him?

- Because praise invites God into your surroundings. Praise invites God to take control of your day, making it pleasurable. You should praise God because He is worthy of all praise.

  "[12]...saying with a loud voice: "Worthy is the Lamb who was slain To receive power and riches and wisdom, and strength and honor and glory and blessing!" Revelation 5.12

Following is a list of principles concerning praise and worship:

- God does not need your praise. If God needed your praise before He could act, then He would be limited by it.

- Praise does not change God.
- Praise changes and affects your life.
- Praise attracts God to your surroundings, in such a way that you will feel confident and able to overcome any adverse situation.
- Praise changes every impossible situation into victories.
- Praise, based on faith, gives thanks to God for the things that He plans to do, before He does them.
- You should begin and end each prayer with praise and worship.
- To praise is to seek God and to worship is to be found by Him. The goal of praise is to create an atmosphere that enables God's presence to descend upon us.
- Praise is initiated by you. Worship is the answer that God gives in response to your praise.
- Praise is something that you do. Worship is something that God loosens.
- Praise is the structure that you build; it is God's house. Worship is when God moves into that house.
- We can not generate worship because it is completely dependent on God.
- We can waltz right into worship through praise; it is God's perogotive to respond to our initiative.

Pre-requisites needed to dwell in His presence

- **Truth and purity** – God is looking for true worshippers. He is looking for people whose words and actions are in harmony with their hearts. *"[8]These people draw near to Me with their mouth, and honor Me with their lips, but their heart is far from Me." Matthew 15.8*

  "[3]Who may ascend into the hill of the LORD? Or who may stand in His holy place? [4]He who has clean hands and a pure heart, who has not lifted up his soul to an idol, nor sworn deceitfully. [5]He shall receive blessing from the LORD, and righteousness from the God of his salvation. [6]This is Jacob, the generation of those who seek Him, who seek Your face." Psalms 24.3-6

- **Integrity** – God is upright in thought, word and action. Do not come into His presence unless you cleanse your spirit. Worship means to have intimacy with God, and when you do this, He is unwilling to be contaminated with your spirit. Worship is a privilege to those who seek Him in spirit and in truth, and who have clean hands and a pure heart.

  "[23]A time will come, however, indeed it is already here, when the true (genuine) worshipers will worship the Father in spirit and in truth (reality); for the Father is seeking just such people as these as His worshipers. [24]God is a Spirit (a spiritual Being) and those who worship Him must worship Him in spirit and in truth (reality). John 4.23, 24 (amplified Bible)

  "[8]These people honor me with their lips, but their hearts are far from me. [9]They worship me in vain; their teachings are but rules taught by men." Matthew 15.8, 9

Worship is the climax of praise. Seek God until His grace and presence are poured upon you. Your goal should be the glorious manifestacion of God upon all things. Praise helps you to find God and to enjoy Him in the fullness of His splendor.

Every area in your life that the enemy has taken hold of, must be lost when God comes.

God's presence brings:

- **Joy**

  I have found many believers that, for a long time, lost their joy because they have not been in God's presence.

- **Peace and rest**

  Rest means a bodily state characterized by minimal functioning and metabolic activities; freedom from activity or labor; a state of motionlessness or inactivity; a place for resting or lodging; peace of mind or spirit. When God is with you, you are the one delivered from all anxiety and worry as He works.

- **Assurance and deliverance**

  When we are in God's presence, we are secured, strengthened and silenced because He is in control.

  "[20]You shall hide them in the secret place of Your presence From the plots of man; you shall keep them secretly in a pavilion from the strife of tongues." Psalms 31.20

- **It changes your circumstances and it gives you the victory over Satan.**

  If you want God to change your circumstances, then begin to praise Him. God will move on your behalf and the enemy will be defeated.

  God's presence is the answer to your every need. The goal is to continually live in God's presence.

  Praise and worship is the first kind of prayer needed to begin your prayer time with God. You will now learn the different types of prayers that can be used during your devotional time to sucessfully increase your time, from only a few minutes to an hour, or longer. You have already learned about the prayer of praise and worship, now you will learn the other ten.

II. The prayer of petition or supplication

This is the kind of prayer that you use when you ask God for your personal needs or desires; to ask for anything that has to do with you and not others. For example: the personal desire to own a house, a new car, a spiritual gift or the need for a friend. As long as the desire of your heart is in line with God's Word, then He will answer you.

The prayer of petition should always go together with thanksgiving. You must keep in mind that this prayer of petition or supplication, in other Bible verses, is called the prayer of faith. The prayer of faith is spoken specifically to ask for personal needs or wants. These could include a new job, health, a promotion at work, a salary increase, a spouse, children, and many others.

"[6]Be anxious for nothing, but in everything by prayer and supplication, with thanksgiving, let your requests be made known to God." Philippians 4.6

"[24]Therefore I say to you, whatever things you ask when you pray, believe that you receive them, and you will have them." Mark 11.24

If you are feeling anxious over a personal matter, then go before God's presence right now! Place your prayer of petition before His throne of grace and God will answer you.

III. The prayer of intercession

The prayer of intercession is to petition or ask God for something, on someone else's behalf. This kind of prayer is where you stand in the gap for others; you raise a cover of protection over another person; you enclose them with your prayers.

As previously stated, the prayer of praise has to do with honoring, glorifing, admiring and celebrating God for who He is and for His great works. The prayer of petition has to do with asking for yourself, and the prayer of intercession is when you ask on someone else's behalf. Every one knows people who are in need, and everyone needs something, which needs prayer and intercession. Let us begin to pray and intercede today!

What are the most important reasons why the Word of God commands that we intercede?

- To intercede for the people in authority.

  "[1]Therefore I exhort first of all that supplications, prayers, intercessions, and giving of thanks be made for all men, [2]for kings and all who are in authority, that we may lead a quiet and peaceable life in all godliness and reverence. [3]For this is good and acceptable in the sight of God our Savior." 1 Timothy 2.1-3

In the verse that you just read, you are asked and encouraged to pray for every spiritual leader in the church and in government, regardless if his or her position is social or political. You should also intercede for your president, congress, representatives, mayors, commissioners, pastors and their families, and church leaders. This prayer of intercession is pleasing to God.

The prayer of intercession is not a selfish prayer because it does not focus on self; it is targeted towards others who are in need of God's favor. The prayer of intercession is also known as the prayer in the spirit or praying in other tongues. We can practice this prayer in two different ways:

1. **With understanding**
2. **In the Spirit or in other tongues**

Let us see what the Bible says on this subject:

"14For if I pray in a tongue, my spirit prays, but my understanding is unfruitful. 15What is the conclusion then? I will pray with the spirit, and I will also pray with the understanding. I will sing with the spirit, and I will also sing with the understanding."
1 Corinthians 14.14, 15

Amplified Bible:

"14For if I pray in an [unknown] tongue, my spirit [by the Holy Spirit within me] prays, but my mind is unproductive [it bears no fruit and helps nobody]. 15Then what am I to do? I will pray with my spirit [by the Holy Spirit that is within me], but I will also pray [intelligently] with my mind and understanding; I will sing with my spirit [by the Holy Spirit that is within me], but I will sing [intelligently] with my mind and understanding also."

When you pray with understanding, which is in your own language, you are praying intelligently, according to God's Word, because you are citing Scripture. But, when you pray in unknown tongues, it is the Spirit, through us, who prays God's perfect will for all the saints.

What are the benefits of praying in other tongues?

1. **You edify yourself.**

The word "edify" in Greek is *"oikodomes"*, which means to construct or build a house or home. Figuratively speaking, this term is used in the New Testament to mean edification or spiritual promotion; it promotes the believer's character. Also, "edify" means to establish or to build upon a foundation.

"4He who speaks in a tongue edifies himself, but he who prophesies edifies the church." 1 Corinthians 14.4

What the Word is saying in this verse is that everytime you pray in unknown tongues, what you are doing is placing another brick on the foundation. What this does within your spirit is to improve who you are; it improves your character. In other words, when you pray in unknown tongues, you experience a spiritual promotion in maturity on the inside. After you pray for one hour, in tongues, you will never be the same again. God will make changes in your spiritual structure and He will promote you to higher levels.

"20But you, beloved, building yourselves up on your most holy faith, praying in the Holy Spirit." Jude 1.20

One more thing that happens when you pray abundantly, in the spirit, is that you feel spiritually charged. It has been my experience that when I finish praying, I feel like a surge of power is poured into me, and this, in turn, enables me to pray for others.

2. **We pray God's perfect will.**

When you pray in the spirit, you pray God's perfect will for His saints. What you have to do now is to ask the Holy Spirit to help you and to guide you to know who you should pray for, what you should ask for and for how long. Surely the Holy Spirit will lead you by the hand and guide your prayers in line with God's perfect will.

If you do not know who to pray for, or what to ask on their behalf, then begin to pray in the Spirit. Lay down your concerns before the Lord; continue talking and praying to Him in His language.

3. **You pray directly to God and not to men.**

Praying in tongues is a direct line of comunication between our spirit and God. Once you establish this line of comunication with God, He will begin to reveal to you the misteries that can only be understood by the Lord.

"2For he who speaks in a tongue does not speak to men but to God, for no one understands him; however, in the spirit he speaks mysteries." 1 Corinthians 14.2

4. **When you pray in the spirit, or in unknown tongues, you exalt and glorify God.**

 "[44]While Peter was still speaking these words, the Holy Spirit fell upon all those who heard the word. [45]And those of the circumcision who believed were astonished, as many as came with Peter, because the gift of the Holy Spirit had been poured out on the Gentiles also. [46]For they heard them speak with tongues and magnify God." Acts 10.44-46

 Everytime we sing or pray in tongues, we are magnifying, exalting, glorifying and honoring God because we are speaking in a heavenly language.

5. **When you pray in tongues, you receive spiritual rest.**

 You receive rest when you pray in tongues because you no longer have to make the effort to attain God's grace and favor. When you speak in tongues the Holy Spirit guides you to pray God's perfect will.

 "[11]For with stammering lips and another tongue He will speak to this people, [12] to whom He said, "This is the rest with which You may cause the weary to rest," and, "This is the refreshing"; yet they would not hear." Isaiah 28.11-12

 It is important to speak in other tongues because this heavenly language makes your prayers effective.

How can you receive the baptism of the Holy Spirit with the evidence of speaking in other tongues?

1. **You need to be born again.** This means that you must first, repent of all your sins, second, invite Jesus into your

heart, and third, you must confess Jesus as the Lord and Savior of your life.

"3Jesus answered and said to him, "Most assuredly, I say to you, unless one is born again, he cannot see the kingdom of God." John 3.3

2. **You must believe that this gift belongs to you.** Every believer who wants to receive the Baptism of the Holy Spirit, with the evidence of speaking in tongues, must believe that he can receive it because this gift is for those who choose to believe, not for unbelievers. This gift is part of the gift of salvation and it is God's will that you receive it right now.

   "17And these signs will follow those who believe: In My name they will cast out demons; they will speak with new tongues." Mark 16.17

   "39For the promise is to you and to your children, and to all who are afar off, as many as the Lord our God will call." Acts 2.39

   You can be a born-again believer, but if you choose not to believe, then these signs are not for you. Notice what Jesus said, *"These signs will follow those who believe?"*

3. **You have to want it.** You must be hungry for the supernatural. You must want and desire the rivers of living water to flow through you.

   "37On the last day, that great day of the feast, Jesus stood and cried out, saying, "If anyone thirsts, let him come to Me and drink. 38He who believes in Me, as the Scripture has said, out of his heart will flow rivers of living water." John 7.37, 38

4. **You have to ask for it.** You must ask for every blessing that God has in store for you and one of these many blessings is the baptism of the Holy Spirit. Open your mouth and say, "Heavenly Father, I want the gift of speaking in other

tongues, give me the fullness of your Holy Spirit right now, in the name of Jesus. Amen!"

"13 If you then, being evil, know how to give good gifts to your children, how much more will your heavenly Father give the Holy Spirit to those who ask Him!" Luke 11.13

5. **The Holy Spirit will give you the gift of speaking in other tongues, but you have to open your mouth and speak.** Many people want the baptism of the Holy Spirit, but they don't make the effort to open their mouths and begin to pronounce what is in their spirit. You must remember that God will give you the gift, but it is up to you to speak by opening your mouth and uttering the words.

"4 And they were all filled with the Holy Spirit and began to speak with other tongues, as the Spirit gave them utterance." Acts 2.4

The same way that you received your salvation, by faith and grace, is the same way you will be filled with the Holy Spirit.

A few aspects of the baptism of the Holy Spirit:

The Word teaches that the baptism in the Holy Spirit and the baptism in water are completely separate from the gift of salvation. After you are born again, there is still another experience waiting for you, and this is operating in the supernatural, which can only be accomplished after you receive the baptism in the Holy Spirit.

"11 I indeed baptize you with water unto repentance, but He who is coming after me is mightier than I, whose sandals I am not worthy to carry. He will baptize you with the Holy Spirit and fire." Matthew 3.11

When you are baptized in the Spirit, you receive supernatural tongues or languages as the evidence that you did receive the gift. Along with this spiritual language you also receive supernatural power. This power gives you the ability to become a better witness for Jesus and it makes you bold when you have to be a witness and testify of His love. Every believer who wants to speak in other tongues can do it because the gift is available for everyone who believes. The only requirement needed to receive the gift is to open up your heart, believe and act upon that belief right now.

IV. The prayer of consecration or dedication.

"39He went a little farther and fell on His face, and prayed, saying, "O My Father, if it is possible, let this cup pass from Me; nevertheless, not as I will, but as You will." Matthew 26.39

In this kind of prayer the believer takes the opportunity to repent and confess any sin that he or she might have committed. Also, this prayer can be used to dedicate and consacrate the areas of your life that have become obstacles in your spiritual life to God.

Everybody offends God either by the spoken word, a thought or action. It is because we are sinners that we need God to cleanse us with His blood every day. Everytime you wake up, and after spending time with God in praise and worship, you should present your petitions before Him. Once you have done this, you should make the prayer of dedication and consecration. In simpler terms, confess every sin that you have committed, repent of your sins and walk away from them.

Also, when you make your prayer of dedication and consecration, you present to God the areas of your life that need change. You should hand over to the Lord your bad character, mood swings, anger, fears, insecurities, doubt, incredulity, impure desires and thoughts. When you make this prayer of dedication and consecration you are making a covenant or commitment to God to improve in those areas which you recognize that you need to change, and your commitment is to be upheld on a daily basis. You should go before God's presence everyday and be accountable for your every action.

It took Jesus a long time to consecrate His will to the Father. He had to pray three times for the same thing until it was settled in His Spirit. You have to do the same thing. You need to sanctify and consecrate your will to the Father everyday until you attain victory.

V. The prayer of thanksgiving

In this kind of prayer you express your thankfulness to God for everything, including past, present and future blessings.

"4Enter into His gates with thanksgiving, and into His courts with praise. Be thankful to Him, and bless His name." Psalms 100.4

This kind of prayer should be continuously in your mouth and heart. The opposite of being thankful is to complain and murmur, which is an act of irreverence to God.

Many people say, "I can't give thanks to God because I am dealing with a huge problem right now," or "I can't be thankful if I don't feel it." However, the Word of God teaches that we should be thankful at all times.

"3I thank my God upon every remembrance of you." Philippians 1.3

When should you express thankfulness to God?

You should tell God how thankful you are everyday. You should do it in the morning, in the afternoon, at night, when you wake up and before you go to sleep. In other words, give thanks to God all of the time.

What should you be thankful for?

You must learn to be thankful for everything. This means that regardless of the situation, crisis or hardship you might be going through, you need to give thanks to God. This includes being thankful for *past, present and future blessings.* When you do this, you learn to be grateful and thankful, remembering His faithfulness and grace.

"18...in everything give thanks; for this is the will of God in Christ Jesus for you." 1 Thessalonias 5.18

There are many blessings for which you could be thankful, for instance, a physical miracle, a house, a car or an offering. I am sure that if you take a moment to think about this you will find something for which you can give thanks to God.

There are certain personal blessings that you will not see manifest until you begin to give thanks; these would be the *future blessings.* Before you receive the answer to your prayers, you should be giving thanks for the answer. Our thankfulness is the same as a prayer of faith, they bring forth the miracle. You must confess your healing, protection, deliverance and health every day, at all times, and you should do it with a thankful heart.

"20giving thanks always for all things to God the Father in the name of our Lord Jesus Christ." Ephesians 5.20

VI. The prayer of waiting upon God

In this kind of prayer, you keep silent before God and wait on Him.

"[7]Rest in the LORD, and wait patiently for Him; do not fret because of him who prospers in his way, because of the man who brings wicked schemes to pass." Psalms 37.7

This is probably the hardest thing for many believers to do because most people love to talk, and talk, and talk, but they can't be quiet for a moment. To be silent before God is very important because God needs to be able to talk to us during this time.

What is the purpose for remaining silent?

During these moments of silence, you give God the opportunity to speak to you. It is very important for you to remember that prayer is a dialogue, not a monologue. Every time you talk to God in prayer, you need to be silent for a moment and give God an opportunity to speak to you and give yourself the opportunity to hear His voice. As you wait for the answer to your prayer, which is already in God's hands, meditate and contemplate upon His greatness and beauty. As you wait in holy silence, waiting for Him to speak, it allows you to see His glory, it allows God to work in your life and it helps you to be closer to Him. This is the time when you give God permission to do as He wills in your life.

VII. The prayer to bind and loosen

"[18]And I also say to you that you are Peter, and on this rock I will build My church, and the gates of Hades shall not prevail against it. [19]And I will

give you the keys of the kingdom of heaven, and whatever you bind on earth will be bound in heaven, and whatever you loose on earth will be loosed in heaven." Matthew 16.18, 19

In this kind of prayer, the believer uses his authority, given by God, against the enemy.

Bind – means to prohibit; to declare something to be ilegal or improper; to declare something ilegitimate. When you are facing the attack of the enemy against your family, finances and children, it is time to use the authority that God has given you. You need to prohibit, bind, declare illegal and improper, everything that the devil is doing against you. When you excersice your authority the devil has to run from you.

Loosen – this word means to be delivered; to open; to allow; to declare something legitimate and legal. You use your authority the same way to bind and to loosen something. This process allows you to establish the kingdom of Heaven on earth and to declare it legal by delivering the oppressed, opening the doors of the captives and letting go of those who are now held in bondage by the enemy. You can do these things when you pray the prayer to bind and loosen.

VIII. The prayer of agreement

"19 Again I say to you that if two of you agree on earth concerning anything that they ask, it will be done for them by My Father in heaven." Matthew 18.19

This is the prayer where two or more believers stand in agreement before the Lord. The prayer of agreement should be practiced with the family and with the brothers and sisters around you.

The meaning of the word **"agreement"** is very interesting. In Greek this word is *"symphoneo"* and it is divided into two words: ***Sym***, which means together, and ***phoneo***, which means to play. Therefore, *"symphoneo"* means to play something simultaneously; in harmony. This word comes from the root word "sinfonia", which is the action of playing something simultaneously. In other words, the word "agreement" means to believe and to speak the same thing. When two or more people stand in agreement, they should receive healing the same way; this is confessing and speaking the same thing.

What steps should you take to pray the prayer of agreement?

1. **Look for someone you can pray with.** The person that you choose to stand in agreement with you should have the same level of faith as you or greater.

2. **Agree on what you will be praying for.** You need to be specific and clear on what you and the other person want to ask God. For example, you both need to agree on the fact that both of you want a 2002 black car, with air conditioning.

3. **After praying and presenting your petitions to God, you need to confess what you asked for and give thanks continuously.** This is what we call harmony. Once you agree on the fact that you want a black car, you must believe, confess and declare the same thing. Also, both of you need to confess that you will receive the same thing you asked God in prayer.

4. **Give God thanks for the answer.** You and the person who stood in agreement with you need to give thanks to God and

begin to declare the same thing concerning what you asked and what you expect to receive.

The prayer of agreement is so powerful that the enemy will try everything, including cause division in the family, because he knows that when a husband and wife agree on something, the results will be powerful.

IX. The prayer of wisdom and revelation

"16do not cease to give thanks for you, making mention of you in my prayers: 17that the God of our Lord Jesus Christ, the Father of glory, may give to you the spirit of wisdom and revelation in the knowledge of Him, 18the eyes of your understanding being enlightened; that you may know what is the hope of His calling, what are the riches of the glory of His inheritance in the saints." Ephesians 1.16-18

In this prayer the believer asks God for wisdom and revelation in Him. I practice this prayer everyday because it is very important for us to want to understand and know the Word of God more and more each day. When you pray this prayer, your understanding will increase and the Lord will begin to reveal hidden truths that can not be perceived by human methods.

What is revelation?

The word "revelation" in Greek is the word *"apokalipsis"*, which means to undress; to remove the veil from a hidden truth; it is to see something in Scripture that was not seen before.

"13 When Jesus came into the region of Caesarea Philippi, He asked His disciples, saying, "Who do men say that I, the Son of Man, am?" Matthew 16.13

The revelation of the Word of God always comes into the heart and not the mind. Each revelation that God gives allows for us to operate in it, using the keys of the kingdom. This will fill us with power and authority to bind and loosen. For this reason, it is very important for you to practice this kind of prayer in which God will have the opportunity to give you the spirit of wisdom and revelation. The enemy will always want to keep you away from any revealed truth because he knows that if you receive knowledge in any area, you will have the keys to the kingdom and the understanding that whatever you bind on earth will be bound in heaven.

Revelation places the keys of the kingdom in your hands and it gives you the authority to bind and loosen; to close and open; to allow and to prohibit on earth and in heaven. Every believer that practices this kind of prayer will receive revelation in the Word, and as the revelation is received, the enemy will not be able to defeat them because they will no longer be ignorant as to the Word or his skeems. If you receive the revelation of what deliverance means, you will have a key to the kingdom that makes the way for you to be free and completely delivered in that area. Pray the prayer to bind and loosen everyday and you will begin to walk in light of the Word.

X. Corporal prayer

In this kind of prayer, the entire congregation or a group of people stand in agreement for a specific purpose.

'[24]So when they heard that, they raised their voice to God with one accord and said: "Lord, You are God, who made heaven and earth and the sea, and all that is in them." Acts 4.24

"[31]And when they had prayed, the place where they were assembled together was shaken; and they were all filled with the Holy Spirit, and they spoke the word of God with boldness." Acts 4.31

How is corporal prayer done?

In unity. When people come together of one accord, one mind, and one purpose to intercede, the result is a powerful move of God. One thing that will make God manifest Himself in all of His glory and splendor is unity. Understanding this should motivate us to keep the unity; we should seek and ask for it in prayer.

"[1]Behold, how good and how pleasant it is for brethren to dwell together in unity! [2]It is like the precious oil upon the head, running down on the beard, the beard of Aaron, running down on the edge of his garments."
Psalms 133.1, 2

XI. The prophetic prayer

This kind of prayer is used to declare, confess and decree, through the leading of the Holy Spirit, the Word of God, His plans and purpose.

How can you pray the prophetic prayer?

- **With the leading of the Holy Spirit.** The Holy Spirit will guide you to pray for the things that you want or need at a specific time. A prophetic prayer is a proclamation and a decree of God's will on earth.

  "[14]For as many as are led by the Spirit of God, these are sons of God. [15]For you did not receive the spirit of bondage again to fear, but

you received the Spirit of adoption by whom we cry out, "Abba, Father." Romans 8.14, 15

- **Confess and declare the Scripture with understanding.**

"3And He said to me, 'Son of man, can these bones live?' So I answered, 'O Lord GOD, You know.' 4Again He said to me, 'Prophesy to these bones, and say to them, 'O dry bones, hear the word of the LORD!' 5Thus says the Lord GOD to these bones: 'Surely I will cause breath to enter into you, and you shall live. 6I will put sinews on you and bring flesh upon you, cover you with skin and put breath in you; and you shall live. Then you shall know that I am the LORD.' 7So I prophesied as I was commanded; and as I prophesied, there was a noise, and suddenly a rattling; and the bones came together, bone to bone. 8Indeed, as I looked, the sinews and the flesh came upon them, and the skin covered them over; but there was no breath in them. 9Also He said to me: "Prophesy to the breath, prophesy, son of man, and say to the breath: 'Thus says the Lord GOD: 'Come from the four winds, o breath, and breathe on these slain, that they may live.'" Ezekiel 37.3-9

The spoken Word has great power. The Word of God brings forth life when you prophesy; when you proclaim it and speak it into that which is lifeless; to broken marriages; to sick bodies and to failed businesses. You are what you declare in prayer that you are; therefore, begin to declare the Word every day. Speak to your body and declare it healed because by His stripes you are healed. Speak, declare and prophesy to everything that goes against God's Word.

You can pray the prophetic prayer with the leading of the Holy Spirit or with understanding in the Word of God, declaring and establishing a decree based on God's Word concerning the situation at hand or when you seek a blessing that is in line with His Word.

XII. The prayer of praise and worship

This kind of prayer is used to praise and worship God. You use it to express your adoration for Him; for who He is and for what He does. To read more about this kind of prayer you can refer back to the beginning of chapter VI where you will find a full detailed description.

Before I close this chapter, I would like to emphasize the following: every time you pray, you should begin and end the prayer with praise and worship. If you pray each prayer for five minutes a day, you will find that your prayer time will increase from minutes into at least an hour. Also, when you choose to make a solid commitment, to discipline yourself, to persevere in prayer and to practice the twelve kinds of prayers that you learned about in this chapter, you will develop a strong prayer life that is continous and persevering. Begin to pray today and receive God's blessings!

8

Fasting and Prayer: A Lifestyle Choice

What is fasting?

Fasting is the voluntary abstention of eating for a determined period of time. This is done for the purpose of seeking God's face and to establish a stronger relationship with Him.

"[12] "Now, therefore," says the LORD, "Turn to Me with all your heart, with fasting, with weeping, and with mourning." Joel 2.12

The word "turn" means to turn back to the starting point; to return and to seek God's face. To return to God, you need to do it wholeheartedly, in fasting and supplication. Today's society is corrupt. Children are more rebellious then ever. Lack of integrity is widespread. There is a crisis concerning moral values and sin is everywhere. None of these things will ever change unless we practice fasting and prayer.

"[16]Moreover, **when** *you fast, do not be like the hypocrites, with a sad countenance. For they disfigure their faces that they may appear to men to be fasting. Assuredly, I say to you, they have their reward. [17]But you, when you fast, anoint your head and wash your face, [18]so that you do not appear to men to be fasting, but to your Father who is in the secret place; and your Father who sees in secret will reward you openly. Matthew 6.16-18*

"When" implies that you can fast and pray whenever you want, without the need for a specific word from God or anyone else that tells us to do it. Fasting and prayer was a way of life for the early church and it should be the same for the church today.

"5…in stripes, in imprisonments, in tumults, in labors, in sleeplessness, in fastings; 6by purity, by knowledge, by longsuffering, by kindness, by the Holy Spirit, by sincere love." 2 Corinthians 6.5, 6 (Paul)

"1 Now in the church that was at Antioch there were certain prophets and teachers: Barnabas, Simeon who was called Niger, Lucius of Cyrene, Manaen who had been brought up with Herod the tetrarch, and Saul. 2As they ministered to the Lord and fasted, the Holy Spirit said, "Now separate to Me Barnabas and Saul for the work to which I have called them." 3Then, having fasted and prayed, and laid hands on them, they sent them away." Acts 13.1-3 (apostles)

The most important thing to remember from the verses that you just read is to practice fasting and prayer as a lifestyle choice. In other words, commit yourself to fast at least once or twice a week, one a month or once every two months. The kind of fasting that you do depends on you. A fast can be partial, absolute or total. Do not wait for God to inspire you to fast. Jesus said, "When you fast," this means that it is up to you when to fast.

What are the three kinds of biblical fasting?

1. **Total** – this fast is accomplished without eating solid foods or drinking any liquids, including water. You will find that in the book of Esther, the Jews did not "eat or drink."

2. **Absolute** – in this fast you do not eat solid foods, but you can drink water. In Matthew 4.1-11 it says, *"2And when He had fasted forty days and forty nights, afterward He was hungry."* It

says that Jesus was hungry; it does not say that He did not eat or drink nor does it say that He was thirsty.

3. **Partial** – this kind of fasting is done by eliminating a certain kind of solid food and or drink from the usual daily diet, as it was in the case of Daniel.

   "[3]I ate no pleasant food, no meat or wine came into my mouth, nor did I anoint myself at all, till three whole weeks were fulfilled."
   Daniel 10.3

   Also, the partial fast is accomplished when you supress one or two meals a day, such as breakfast and lunch, or when you choose to eat only fruit or vegetables.

What is the purpose of fasting?

There are seven reasons why you should fast:

1. **To honor God.** You honor God when you choose to dedicate a certain amount of time to spend with Him and to seek His face. This time is dedicated only to God. During this time, you recognize who God is and you give Him the place of honor that He deserves.

2. **To humble and repent before His presence.** It is not often that we realize how prideful we are. Arrogance and humbleness are misteries. People do not walk around saying "I am prideful" or "I am humble." Pride and humbleness are conditions of the heart; it is who we are. The only time that it is evident to us that we have pride or lack humbleness is when we fast and pray; it allows us to see our true self.

“1Now on the twenty-fourth day of this month the children of Israel were assembled with fasting, in sackcloth, and with dust on their heads. 2Then those of Israelite lineage separated themselves from all foreigners; and they stood and confessed their sins and the iniquities of their fathers.” Nehemiah 9.1, 2

When you fast God will show you if you have pride. He can humble you in private or in public. If God humbles you in public the humiliation will last longer because your instinct will be to resist. If God humbles you in private the humiliation will not last as long because the request to know was initiated by you and not by Him.

“15For thus says the High and Lofty One who inhabits eternity, whose name is Holy: "I dwell in the high and holy place, with him who has a contrite and humble spirit, to revive the spirit of the humble, and to revive the heart of the contrite ones.” Isaiah 57.15

The Word of God exhorts you to prove if you have faith. How can you do this? You know you have faith when you humble yourself in the presence of God as you fast and pray.

3. **To face a crisis.** Every time you have to face a crisis, when you are going through the deserts in your life, when you are tempted or dealing with financial adversity, marital problems or trying to overcome the obstacles that the enemy has raised up before you, it is time to fast and pray.

“1It happened after this that the people of Moab with the people of Ammon, and others with them besides the Ammonites, came to battle against Jehoshaphat. 2Then some came and told Jehoshaphat, saying, "A great multitude is coming against you from beyond the sea, from Syria; and they are in Hazazon Tamar" (which is En Gedi). 3And

Jehoshaphat feared, and set himself to seek the LORD, and proclaimed a fast throughout all Judah." 2 Chronicles 20.1-3

When the great armies of the enemy surround you, it is time to fast and pray. Every time you face a major crisis in your life you must declare war against the enemy with fasting and prayer.

4. **To hear His voice and to ask for direction.**

   "[3]He restores my soul; He leads me in the paths of righteousness for His name's sake." Psalms 23.3

   Many times you might find yourself in difficult situations. You will have no idea how you should act; do you strike the rock or do you speak to it; do you take authority or do you wait on God. If fasting and prayer is a lifestyle choice for you, then you will be able to hear God's voice.

5. **To ordain people into the ministry.** Fasting and prayer should always be the first thing that a leader does when he needs to separate a man or a woman for the work of the ministry. God takes this matter very seriously; it is very important.

   "[1]Now in the church that was at Antioch there were certain prophets and teachers: Barnabas, Simeon who was called Niger, Lucius of Cyrene, Manaen who had been brought up with Herod the tetrarch, and Saul. [2]As they ministered to the Lord and fasted, the Holy Spirit said, "Now separate to Me Barnabas and Saul for the work to which I have called them." [3]Then, having fasted and prayed, and laid hands on them, they sent them away." Acts 13.1-3

6. **To develop spiritual sensitivity.** When you fast your spiritual perception and sensitivity is sharpened. If there was something in the Word that you did not understand, after you fast and pray, your understanding in the Word will increase. If it is difficult to hear the voice of God, after you fast and pray, you will be able to hear it with ease. Witches, spiritist and Satanists fast against the church. According to them, fasting makes more evil spirits to come to their aid, thus increasing their power. If these people fast to increase their evil power, imagine how great God's power will be, in you, when you fast and pray!

7. **To lose the bonds of wickedness.**

"[6]Is this not the fast that I have chosen: to loose the bonds of wickedness, to undo the heavy burdens, to let the oppressed go free, and that you break every yoke?" Isaiah 58.6

As stated earlier, "to loose" in Hebrew means to open a door that was closed; to deliver someone from captivity; to loosen a prisioner; to untie a knot. There are traps and obstacles that the enemy sends into your life that are impossible to break, except through fasting and prayer. The only way to open a door that was closed, perhaps in your business, workplace, ministry, marriage, health or others, is through fasting and prayer.

What steps should you take to fast?

1. **You must declare your fast before God in an audible voice.** When you do this, ask God what kind of fasting you should follow: absolute, partial or total. Also, determine how long you are going to do it and confess with your mouth the moment that you start your fast.

2. **Define the purpose for your fast.** What is the reason you are declaring a fast? You can have more then one reason for fasting, but before you begin you must be specific with God. For example: "Lord, I declare this fast for my children's salvation."

3. **Ask the Holy Spirit to help you.** The Holy Spirit is our comforter and counselor. Ask Him to give you the spiritual, physical and emotional strength that you will need as you do your fast; He *will* help to keep you strong. This is a very important point because many people are tempted to end their fast, but if you ask the Holy Spirit's help before the temptation comes, He will be there for you.

4. **Receive the answer to your fast before it comes.** *"Your Father who sees in secret will Himself reward you openly."*

   "16Moreover, when you fast, do not be like the hypocrites, with a sad countenance. For they disfigure their faces that they may appear to men to be fasting. Assuredly, I say to you, they have their reward. 17But you, when you fast, anoint your head and wash your face."
   Matthew 6.16, 17

You should give thanks to God for receiving the answer to your petition during your fast and prayer before you see it manifest in the natural. It is important to keep in mind that this is not a business transaction with God, rather, the answer to your prayer comes as a result of your diligence in searching for Him, and because you want to be closer to Him, He will reward you. God always rewards those who diligently seek Him.

To close this subject we can conclude that fasting and prayer go together. When believers fast and pray with the right heart-felt attitude, with the correct intentions, and in line with God's Word, the results are powerful.

Fasting and prayer is a powerful tool in the hands of believers, but it does not change God; it changes you. Fasting is one way to enjoy the presence of God. Also, it should be a lifestyle choice for every believer and it should not be done once in a while, otherwise, the results will not be the same. Regardless of what kind of fasting you choose to do, the results will be wonderful; as long as you do it continuously.

9

How to Pray for Our Unbelieving Family

Any one who truly understands what hell is like would not want to go there. It is a place of torment. The Word of God describes it as a place where the worm never dies and the fire is never quenched. Every person who chooses not to receive Jesus as their Lord and Savior will go to this place of torment. Many people wonder why so many are unable to see the truth of the gospel, they ask questions such as: "What is preventing them from receiving the gospel?" "Could it be that God does not want to save them?" "Is there something standing in the way of them believing in the truth of Jesus?"

Before learning this topic, first allow us to explain what God's desire is for His people.

God wants everyone to receive salvation.

"9The Lord is not slack concerning His promise, as some count slackness, but is longsuffering toward us, not willing that any should perish but that all should come to repentance." 2 Peter 3.9

This verse is powerful. It explains that God's will is that no one should perish. Then, why are so many people lost and ignorant to the truth of Christ, if you and I both know that God's will is to save the world? What is preventing them from believing? One thing is certain, God is not the problem or the obstacle standing in the way of your family's salvation. Then who is at fault?

The Word of God teaches that the world is blinded by the enemy and it is this spiritual blindness that prevents people from seeing and receiving the truth.

"3But even if our gospel is veiled, it is veiled to those who are perishing, 4whose minds the god of this age has blinded, who do not believe, lest the light of the gospel of the glory of Christ, who is the image of God, should shine on them." 2 Corinthians 4.3, 4

Let us now dig deeper into what God is saying to us in these verses. The word **"veilded"** in Greek is *"kalupsis"*, which means hidden; covered up; wrapped up. What does this mean? It means that the unbelievers can not see the light of the gospel because the enemy has the truth hidden from them; he has them veiled or blinded from the truth. However, the power and authority to remove this veil from their minds was given to every believer; to you and me. This word is closely related to the Greek word *"apokalupsis"*, which means revelation; to remove the veil; to strip or undress, to unearth or uncover. In simpler terms, until the unbeliever has a personal encounter and revelation with the gospel of Jesus Christ, he will not know God.

"17Jesus answered and said to him, "Blessed are you, Simon Bar-Jonah, for flesh and blood has not revealed this to you, but My Father who is in heaven." Matthew 16.17

The enemy's goal is to hide the truth of the gospel and to keep the unbelievers in bondage. The revelation is the light that makes the unbeliever understand and be enlightened by the truth. Where there is no revelation, there is no light, and if there is no light, there is darkness.

"4...whose minds the god of this age has blinded, who do not believe, lest the light of the gospel of the glory of Christ, who is the image of God, should shine on them." 2 Corinthians 4.4

The word **"blinded"** in Greek is the word *"tuphloo,"* meaning to darken; to weaken; to dull the intellect and the mind. The root of this word means "to make smoke." The idea behind this word is like a screen of smoke that darkens to the point of complete blindness. There is a veil of darkness that covers the minds of the unbelievers; it was placed by the enemy to prevent them from understanding the gospel.

What is this word teaching us? The reason why people doubt Jesus is because the enemy has darkened their understanding and he has dulled their mind, in such a way that even when they want to see the truth, they can't. Many people around the world are total skeptics to anything having to do with God. They don't want to know about Him because they are blinded by the devil.

What prevents the unbeliever from understanding? **Pride and arrogance in people** makes them reject the advice of others. They refuse to submit to authority and live as they please. They live independently from God because they feel self-sufficient. Selfishness, self-justification and independence are part of pride and arrogance; these are in every human being and the devil uses them to blind the minds of the people.

The wages of a prideful and arrogant person is spiritual blindness.

Love for self, everything that satisfies the ego, exalting everything that has to do with self and any other message that preaches the denial of self is offensive to the ego. What do we have to do to remove the veil from people's minds? We must pray fervently for the root of this pride to be removed completely from our family and the people for whom we pray for, so that they can come to Christ. We must understand that the reason people do not receive Jesus, and they want nothing to do with Him, is because the enemy has them blinded to the truth, in such a way, that they are unable to understand; they are powerless. Then, it is our responsibility to pray for that veil that is blocking the light of the gospel to be removed and for them to receive the truth.

What steps should you take to pray effectively for your family?

1. **You must break the power that blinds them, in the name of Jesus.**

   One thing that you should do to break the power of the enemy is to be specific when you pray and to do it with power. Use the following example as a guide:

   "Heavenly Father, I break the power of the devil that blinds ____________________ (the name of the person) and in the name of Jesus I order you to loosen him/her and to remove the veil that is blinding him/her, right now. I break the power of spiritual blindness, pride and arrogance."

   Sometimes, the power of the enemy will be broken instantaneously, and in others, it will be progressively. Don't give up praying for your family member or friend, even if he or she starts to get worse after you begin to pray. Continue to pray because in the spiritual realm, the power of the devil has already been broken. Believe it wholeheartedly and continue to pray without ceasing!

2. **Pray that God sends workers to the harvest.**

   "2Then He said to them, "The harvest truly is great, but the laborers are few; therefore pray the Lord of the harvest to send out laborers into His harvest." Luke 10.2

   God has everything in abundance except for one thing, workers; and this does not depend on Him, but on the will of men. God does not force anyone to serve Him. If you choose to serve Him it is because you want to do it wholeheartedly.

Before your family can be saved it is necessary for you to pray every day and in your prayers you need to ask God to send people to surround the unbelieving members of your family. You should pray that wherever they are or whatever they are doing or whoever they are with, whether at school or prison, at the hospital or in their business, the people around them will talk to them about Jesus.

I remember that before I met Jesus, everywhere I went there was someone talking to me about Him. When I was at the university, at the barber shop, at the movies, the restaurant, and every where else, people would come up to me and talk to me about Jesus. I believe this happened because there was someone praying for my salvation. Someone, somewhere, broke the power of the devil that was over me and that was holding me captive and in darkness; this prepared the way for me to receive Jesus and my salvation.

3. **Pray that God prepares their hearts and that they may receive the good news of the Gospel.**

"[20]But these are the ones sown on good ground, those who hear the word, accept it, and bear fruit: some thirtyfold, some sixty, and some a hundred." Mark 4.20

You need to pray everyday and ask the Lord to prepare the heart of the people who are unbelievers. Ask the Lord to change his or her heart, making them tender and gentle and for their hearts to be good planting ground so when the seed of the gospel is planted it will bear fruit. Pray for the veil to be removed and for God's Word to be revealed in their hearts.

4. Pray that their repentance is genuine.

> *"[9]The Lord is not slow in keeping his promise, as some understand slowness. He is patient with you, not wanting anyone to perish, but everyone to come to repentance." 2 Peter 3.9*

True repentance is a genuine change of mind, direction and heart. It is a new understanding that comes from God as a result of having a personal revelation. This revelation will produce a change in the individual, not only in attitude, but also in action, direction and lifestyle.

5. Pray that their understanding will be enlightened.

> *"[17]I keep asking that the God of our Lord Jesus Christ, the glorious Father, may give you the Spirit of wisdom and revelation, so that you may know him better. [18]I pray also that the eyes of your heart may be enlightened in order that you may know the hope to which he has called you, the riches of his glorious inheritance in the saints."*
> *Ephesians 1.17, 18*

You should practice the steps that you have just learned everyday. Don't give up regardless of how your family is acting or if the people that you are praying for get worse. Continue to pray until the power of the enemy is broken over their lives and the promise of God is fulfilled. Never lose sight of the fact that the day you received your salvation you also received a promise that automatically included your family. God included this promise as part of His covenant with you the day that you received Him as Lord and Savior.

"[31]They replied, "Believe in the Lord Jesus, and you will be saved--you and your household." Acts 16.31

Do not dismay or give up. Continue to pray for your family. God is faithful to fulfill the promise that He made to you.

10

How to Begin a Ministry of Prayer and Intercession in a Local Church

The ministry of intercession is a very important one for the local church. One thing that God spoke to me about when our church was funded was the need to establish a prayer ministry and to invest in prayer. At the time, it was hard for me to understand why God wanted us to invest money into prayer, but a short time later the Lord cleared this up for me. God said that the way to invest money into the prayer ministry was to include full time intercessors (with a salary) as part of the church staff.

At first, I was greatly criticized. People said that no one should be paid to pray. However, when I was faced with this kind of criticism my answer to these people was "Every workers is worthy of his salary." It is important to remember that the gift of intercession is given by God to the believers, just as He calls some to be pastors, evangelists, prophets, teachers or any other gift mentioned in the Word; these, too, receive a salary.

The ministry of intercession in our church was initiated and established by my wife Ana. She gave birth to it in the Spirit during the early hours of the day. While pregnant with my son Ronald, she would rise in the early hours of the morning to pray. At the time, the church was under construction and sometimes she would be the only one to show up for prayer, but she persevered; this is very important. Praying among the rubble and debris left over by the daily construction work was not a comfortable thing to do, but it was done. This was the beginning of the ministry of intercession; at first, it was only for three hours in the morning. I strongly believe that if you want the members of your congregation to be involved in this ministry, or any other ministry, as leaders, you should be the first to be an example. Otherwise, no one is ever going to be motivated to participate. Today, we have twenty-four hours of continual prayer, which include twelve full-time intercessors; they do it in eight hour shifts per day.

The eight hour shifts are covered by the full-time intercessors, but in addition to them we have over 200 volunteer intercessors that come at different times during the day.

Before the ministry of intercession is established, there are certain questions that should be asked, that will guide and confirm the ministry within the church.

I. What is the purpose for the ministry of intercession to be established in a local church?

a. To build up a spiritual hedge of protection around the church, the families that attend, the pastor and the leaders.

b. Every time the enemy comes against our ministry it has been unveiled and destroyed in prayer and intercession. Sometimes, the intercessors destroy the attacks of the enemy before they can cause any harm to me, the pastor.

Intercession raises up a hedge of protection, a wall, a strong barrier around the church and its members that prevents the enemy from penetrating.

c. To give birth to the things established in the vision of the church and the body of Christ.

"19My dear children, for whom I am again in the pains of childbirth until Christ is formed in you." Galatians 4.19

Most of the blessings that God has given our ministry, which include buildings, properties, television, radio, land, souls, healing, miracles, and more, were birthed in the Spirit through the intercessors. Sometimes the process has taken days, other times weeks, months and years before the evidence is manifested, but the victory has always been ours.

If the local church does not have a ministry of intercession, there will not be any new things to be birthed nor is God's will going to be fulfilled in that ministry.

d. Pray for the needs of the people.

There are many believers defeated, hurt and wounded in the body of Christ; they need someone who will stand in the gap for them. They are unable to defend themselves from the attacks of the enemy; thus the importance of the ministry of intercession.

II. What is the gift of intercession and how can you identify a true intercessor?

One important key for a successful ministry of intercession is to place the right people with the right calling into the right ministry. These people should feel love and be passionate for prayer.

Next, you will learn what the gift of intercession is and what evidence proves that a believer has this gift. Also, you will learn a few of the dangers and the different kind of intercessors that exist.

The gift of intercession

What is the gift of **intercession?** It is the ability given by the Holy Spirit to pray for long periods of time. Furthermore, it means to have great passion for prayer and to stand in the gap before God for the needs of others.

"[30]I looked for a man among them who would build up the wall and stand before me in the gap on behalf of the land so I would not have to destroy it, but I found none." Ezekiel 22.30

What is the **purpose** for the gift of intercession?

- To build up a spiritual protection around the church and the family.
- To stand in the gap between God and men and to fulfill God's will on earth.
- To give birth to what has already been established in the vision of the church and in the body of Christ.
- To make war against the devil and his demons by destroying all of his plans.

What is the evidence that proves that a believer has the gift or the calling for the ministry of intercession?

1. **They pray for long periods of time and enjoy it.**

   When a person loves to pray for many hours without complaining it is evident that a person is an intercessor; they enjoy doing it.

2. **They operate strongly in the gift of discernment of spirits.**

   Intercessors perceive, feel, see and hear in the spirit because they have the gift of discernment of spirits.

3. **Intercessors identify with the burden and pain of other people.**

   When they talk to people, they can perceive if that person has a burden or problem and immediately being to pray for them.

4. **They often see their prayers answered, more than any other average believer.**

   God answers their prayers, even when they are not very specific. The results of their prayers are more powerful than any other believer.

5. **They always have an attitude of prayer.**

   Regardless of where they are or with whom, they are always interceding. The Word of God teaches us to pray without ceasing. This is what happens to the intercessor; he or she is always in prayer.

6. **The gifts of compassion and love are evident in them.**

   This is one sign that is evident in a true intercessor. In other words, love and compasion give the true intercesor sensibility to the needs of other people.

7. **They often experience sensations or symptoms in their physical body, which alerts them to incoming danger.**

   Many intercessors experience the same symptoms of the person or they feel a burden over the situation they are praying for. They might get a headache, backache, the desire to vomit, dizziness, lightheadedness, among many. This usually happens to the intercessors of crisis.

8. **Intercessors are extremely sensitive to the spiritual realm.**

   If they are not careful, they will perceive that which is bad more than what is good.

9. **They have a deep passion for prayer and intercession.**

   The intercessor has the conviction that everything can and will be resolved through prayer. They sincerely believe that there is nothing impossible for God.

10. **Intercessors hate injustice.**

    When the intercessor is a witness to an injustice, his or her heart sympathizes with the victim.

    We could look into more evidence that proves that a person has the genuine call to be an intercessor, but the characteristics which you have just learned are the most common.

What is the danger of the gift of intercession if it is not dealt with properly?

- Intercessors might believe that they are the only ones that can hear from God and that they are the highest authority of God on earth.

- They might believe that they are spiritually superior to others because they spend more time in prayer.

- They could have the tendency to perceive evil more than what is good.

- They might want to manipulate the pastor and the leaders with their prayers.

- They might make prayers of judgment against people.

It is extremely important for every intercessor to submit to a spiritual covering. He or she should never initiate a prayer assignment without the blessing and authority of the pastor or leader.

What different kinds of intercesors exist?

Like any other ministry, there are different kinds of intercessors with a specific calling from God to intercede in a specific area. Let us take a look at the different kinds of intercessors that exist:

1. Intercessors for salvation

These intercessors stand in the gap for the people who need to receive Jesus as their personal Savior. They pray for the unbelievers with moans and groans; they weep and have great passion for the lost. Many times, when God motivates them to pray, they will feel as if they are giving birth to a baby. Their intercession is directed exclusively towards the lost.

Many people will never receive salvation until an intercesor stands in the gap and gives birth to them, in the spirit, through intercession.

2. **Intercessors for finances**

The intercessors for finances have been anointed by God to intercede for the finances of the kingdom. They pray for people to receive the funds needed to spread the gospel; they have abundance of faith to pray for money. This kind of intercessor prays so that the riches of this world will transfer unto the hands of God's children.

3. **Personal intercessors**

Personal intercessors are spiritual guardians that God depends on to present confidential information before His throne as they ask for protection, provision and other priorities that need prayer, whether they have something to do with a person or an individual. Some of these intercessors receive assignments from God to pray for a person or an individual.

Every believer should have a personal intercessor.

4. **Crisis intercessors**

Crisis intercessors are the paramedics of prayer. They go in and out of God's presence with urgent petitions, as they place themselves in the gap for others. They also act as vigilantes for God's people.

As you previously learned, intercessors experience certain symptoms or sensations in their bodies, which warns them of incoming danger, a burden that needs prayer or any urgency that the Holy Spirit might place in their hearts. You, as a crisis intercessor, will receive a burden that needs prayer. Do not stop praying for it until there is a breakthrough in the spirit. This is something few crisis intercessors understand or are aware of. Sometimes, they will pray, but will stop half-way before the breakthrough. Other times, they will have great prayer burdens and pray for weeks, sometimes months, before they see the breakthrough in the spirit.

There is a great intercessor in this country, she is 77 years old. One day she asked the Lord, "Why are you always prompting me to pray for crisis situations only?" And the Lord answered her, "Because many of the young intercessors do not understand that they have to pray until there is a breakthrough. However, if I burden you to pray for a crisis, you don't let go of it until you feel the breakthrough in the spirit." Crisis intercessors have to learn to intercede until there is a breakthrough.

5. Warfare intercessors

These intercessors are the powerful military strength of prayer. They fight to establish God's truth in places where the devil has built a stronghold, in people, in a specific situation, in your home or the nation.

The evidence that proves that a person is a warfare intercessor is that he or she will declare spiritual warfare against the enemy throughout the entire prayer. They also have great authority to respond and to cast out demons.

6. Worship intercessors

Worship intercessors intercede through praise and worship. They prepare the way for the power of God to be poured on the land.

7. Leadership intercessors

Leadership intercessors are people who specialize in interceding for church leaders, such as: the pastor, the family and the rest of the leaders within the body of Christ. They have been assigned by God to intercede specifically for the leadership.

8. Intercessors for the government

These intercessors stand in the gap for government leaders, politicians and influential people in public office.

I strongly believe that every intercessor should pray everyday for the president and his cabinet, but God has also assigned people to pray specifically for these kinds of people.

9. Prophetic intercessors

Prophetic intercessors have the ability to see into the invisible realm and to hear what the human ear is not capable of hearing. They declare God's will for a specific moment and a specific place; they are God's mouthpiece.

10. Intercessors for Israel

God has called a group of intercessors to pray and intercede for Israel. They have a deep passion for the Jewish community and they are able to identify with their pain and needs.

III. How do you look for, and find, a secret place for the ministry of intercession?

What is the secret place?

The secret place is where you meet God every day. It is a place where you enter into His presence and where you are transformed, taught, disciplined and loved. It is a place where you receive restoration, forgiveness and the revelation of your calling. This secret place is the prayer room.

"20You shall hide them in the secret place of Your presence from the plots of man; you shall keep them secretly in a pavilion from the strife of tongues." Psalms 31.20

"6But you, when you pray, go into your room, and when you have shut your door, pray to your Father who is in the secret place; and your Father who sees in secret will reward you openly." Matthew 6.6

Every believer should have a prayer room; a secret place where God can be found everyday. Every church should also have a secret and exclusive prayer room where the intercessors can gather together to pray continually.

All of us can pray anywhere. We can pray at the restaurant, in the airplane, at the hotel, in the street, at the bank, or anywhere we might find ourselves, but there is a great difference when there is a special place designed specifically for prayer and fellowship with God.

Following are several important factors that you should know concerning these "places":

- Places are **important** to God. He created the "places" before He created man and it was the first purpose of the Holy Spirit. *"And the Spirit of God was hovering over the face of the waters."*

- Miracles occur in **specific places.**

  "[4]But He needed to go through Samaria." John 4.4

  When you read the story of the Samaritan woman you begin to understand that Jesus knew in what places miracles would occur. Faith operates stronger in some places more than in others. Faith-filled people have the ability to creat an atmosphere for miracles in towns, cities and nations.

  Doubt can block or stop miracles from happening.

  "[57]So they were offended at Him. But Jesus said to them, 'A prophet is not without honor except in his own country and in his own house.' [58]Now He did not do many mighty works there because of their unbelief." Matthew 13.57, 58

  Naman was healed in the Jordan River and the blind man received his sight at the Pool of Siloam. These were also places where God performed miracles.

  "[6]When He had said these things, He spat on the ground and made clay with the saliva; and He anointed the eyes of the blind man with the clay. [7]And He said to him, "Go, wash in the pool of Siloam" (which is translated, Sent). So he went and washed, and came back seeing." John 9.6, 7

You can create a room or a place that is filled with God's presence. This room should have worship music playing all the time. The Word of God should be written on the walls and it should contain paper and pencil to write down everything that the Lord reveals to the intercessors.

When the room or place for prayer or intercession is chosen it should be sanctified and separated for the exclusive use of the prayer and intercession ministry. Some of the following tools and utensils used should also be included:

- Anointing oil
- Water
- Worship music
- Written prayer petitions
- Paper and pencils
- Soft lighting
- Bread and wine for the Lord's Supper

It is important to be in the right place for miracles to occur.

IV. For how long should you pray?

You can begin by praying for one hour a day. As people begin to join the prayer team, increase the hours until there is prayer twenty-four hours a day, or at least until enough time is dedicated to every need of the people and the church. Our church started with three hours a day and it now covers twenty-four hours. It is important to be clear on the fact that when our church started this ministry of intercession it was done with volunteers until it was included in the church's annual budget; these volunteers then joined the staff on a full time basis.

V. What should be prayed for?

There are certain priorities of prayer and intercession that intercessors should pray for:

1. The pastor and his family

- Divine wisdom
- Spirit of wisdom and revelation
- Protection
- A greater level of anointing
- Fear of God
- Church and personal finances
- Pastor and his family
- Health
- Pastor and his personal finances

2. The vision of the local church

- Souls
- Leadership
- Finances
- The different departments within the church
- God's presence
- Future plans and proyects

3. The body of Christ

- Evangelism
- For God's will to be done on earth
- Pastors and leaders